A lesson a week

The Theory of Guitar
made easy

Vince Inchierca

Vendera Publishing

A LESSON A WEEK:
THE THEORY OF GUITAR MADE EASY
by
VINCE INCHIERCA

Edited by Jaime Vendera, Vince Inchierca, and Paul Koenig
Interior Design by Daniel Middleton (scribefreelance.com)
Cover Design by Molly Burnside (crosssidedesigns.com)
Graphics by Vince Inchierca and Paul Koenig
Proofreading by Angelique Inchierca

ISBN: 978-1-936307-44-9

Copyright © 2017 by Vincent Inchierca, Paul Koenig, and Vendera Publishing

All rights reserved.

This book or any portion thereof may not be reproduced or used in any manner whatsoever without the written permission of the publisher.

Contents

INTRODUCTION 1

CHAPTER ONE: THE BASICS 3
   Before We Get Started 4
   WEEK ONE: NATURAL NOTES ON THE GUITAR NECK 9
   WEEK TWO: BASIC CHORDS IN C MAJOR 20
   WEEK THREE: MODES OF THE C MAJOR SCALE 24
   WEEK FOUR: REVIEW 31

CHAPTER TWO: AN IN-DEPTH STUDY OF CHORDS 32
   Before We Get Started 33
   WEEK FIVE: AN INTRODUCTION TO POWER CHORDS 35
   WEEK SIX: AN INTRODUCTION TO ARPEGGIOS 46
   WEEK SEVEN: THE CIRCLE OF FIFTHS 52
   WEEK EIGHT: REVIEW 55

CHAPTER THREE: EXOTIC SCALES & MODES 56
   Before We Get Started 57
   WEEK NINE: MIXING SCALES & MODES 59
   WEEK TEN: HARMONIC MINOR, MELODIC MINOR & DIMINISHED SCALES 61
   WEEK ELEVEN: CHROMATIC SCALES 66
   WEEK TWELVE: REVIEW 68

CHAPTER FOUR: BLUES VERSUS PENTATONICS 69
   Before We Get Started 70
   WEEK THIRTEEN: BLUES CHORDS & PROGRESSIONS 71
   WEEK FOURTEEN: BASIC PENTATONIC SCALE PATTERNS 81
   WEEK FIFTEEN: MIXING IT UP WITH BLUES SCALES 83
   WEEK SIXTEEN: REVIEW 85
   BOOK REVIEW 86

ABOUT THE AUTHOR 88

INTRODUCTION

Welcome to *A Lesson a Week: The Theory of Guitar Made Easy*. Allow me to take the time to first explain what this book is really about and why you need it. This book is a supplement on learning the theory behind guitar; not actually as a replacement to lessons, but to help with the questions behind learning that might come up during your studies. Therefore, it goes hand-in-hand with your guitar studies, helping to expand your theory knowledge, thus enhancing your overall musicianship.

Guitar theory is a subject that has been made into a problem for many guitar players, but I assure you, it is not an issue. In fact, it can be quite easy and fun to learn guitar theory. If you begin to look at it like it's a language, once you start to learn that language, it becomes like muscle memory; very simplistic to recall upon without thinking, like breathing.

While studying guitar, I found that many teachers, local schools, and books, taught you how to play songs, but only implied or hinted at theory. Schools with classes on theory would usually bog you down with the classical approach. Since I saw a gap that needed to be filled within the instruction of theory, I decided to write a book that will teach you the theory of guitar in a way that you can incorporate theory into your playing, which will enable you to write your own progressions and solos, instead of just copying the same patterns already established by other players.

This book will be broken into of four major chapters, with each chapter broken up into four weeks of theory enlightenment, featuring three weeks of training, followed by a week of review. The idea is to approach each chapter as a weekly learning course, with the final week of each chapter serving as a time to test yourself. Once you have a complete understanding of this material, you should proceed to the next chapter of the book.

When learning guitar, most players get told to, "Learn your neck." That's great advice! You *should* learn the neck of the guitar! Next, you'll usually learn some scales and a whole lot of licks. But without an understanding as to why the scales and licks make sense, a guitarist will easily end up copying ideas from other guitarists who they admire and have learned from. In other words, the guitarist simply becomes a copy of their idols, never quite learning how to stand alone as an individual player in most cases.

My goal is to enhance your playing by expanding your thinking beyond what you learn from the usual standard guitar lessons, so that you have the creative freedom to explore your musical visions and become your own unique guitar player. This book will teach you not only to know your neck, but also to understand the scales and modes from any position on that neck, so that you also understand the theory behind what you are playing, and have a vast repertoire to experiment with your soloing.

Did you know, for instance, there are four scale runs on a standard 24 fret guitar? In just one Major key! (We'll explain in more detail later.) We're going to break it all down so that the mastery of this language of theory is easier than riding a bike. Hopefully this will help you in your musical endeavor.

Before moving on into the lessons, I'd like to share with you a bit about the first chapter and what it contains, so that you're prepared before you start your first week. So, let's move on to the first part of Chapter One.

CHAPTER ONE: THE BASICS

Before we begin Week One, we'll start with a basic explanation of each weekly lesson, as well as cover some questions and terms that apply to your lessons, such as, "What is a fret space on the neck of the guitar?" Study the following weekly breakdown and terms before beginning Week One:

Week One: Natural Notes on the Neck of the Guitar
Week One is an introduction to the key of C Major and the C Major scale, which will go into the teaching of the natural notes, i.e., their basic "Do-Re-Mi..." functions and theory, and a basic outline of natural notes versus sharps and flats.

Week Two: Basic Chords in the C Major Scale
In Week Two, you will learn to break down how chords are made from scales and which are to be used (Major, Minor, and Diminished) from each particular scale.

Week Three: The Modes of the C Major Scale
In Week Three, I'll go through the basic modes and their position to the Major scale. In case you're wondering, the reason we're going to stick with the C Major scale is because all the notes used in the C Major scale are natural notes (with no sharps and no flats). This will make it easier when first learning guitar theory.

Week Four: Review
During the final week of Chapter One, you will review what you've learned from the previous weeks.

Before We Get Started

Here is a quick preface of questions that might arise during the reading of this chapter, since my significant other asked, "What is a fret? & What is a step?" We will assume that you are brand new to guitar for the sake of teaching everyone from the same starting point.

What is a repertoire?
1. A list of musical pieces or parts that a person is prepared to perform.
2. The complete list of musical works available for performance.
3. The complete list of skills, used in a musical practice.

What is fret wire?
A fret wire is the thin metal wire that separates the frets going up and down the length of the neck. If you look at the neck you will see spaces separated by fret wire.

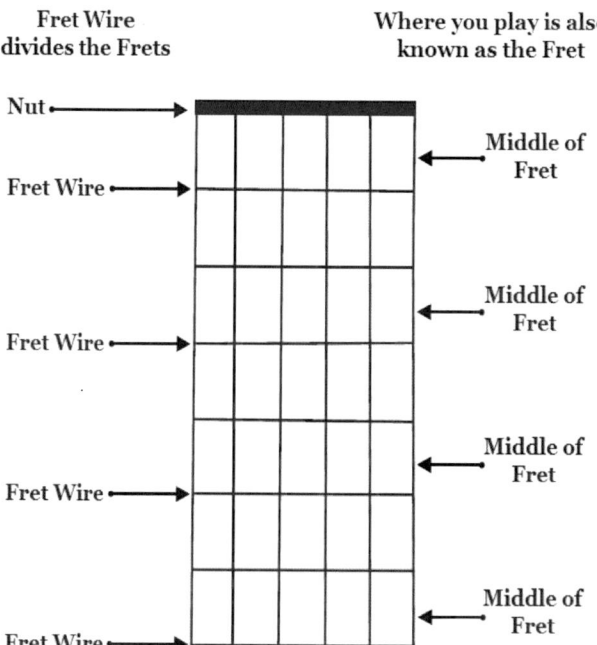

What is a fret?
A fret is the space between the two metal bars across the neck, called fret wire. The first fret is the space between the nut, sometimes white plastic, sometimes metal, and the first fret wire.

What is a step or a space?
A step or a space is the distance between one fret to another. Steps and spaces are the same just using different words.

What is a half-step versus a whole-step?

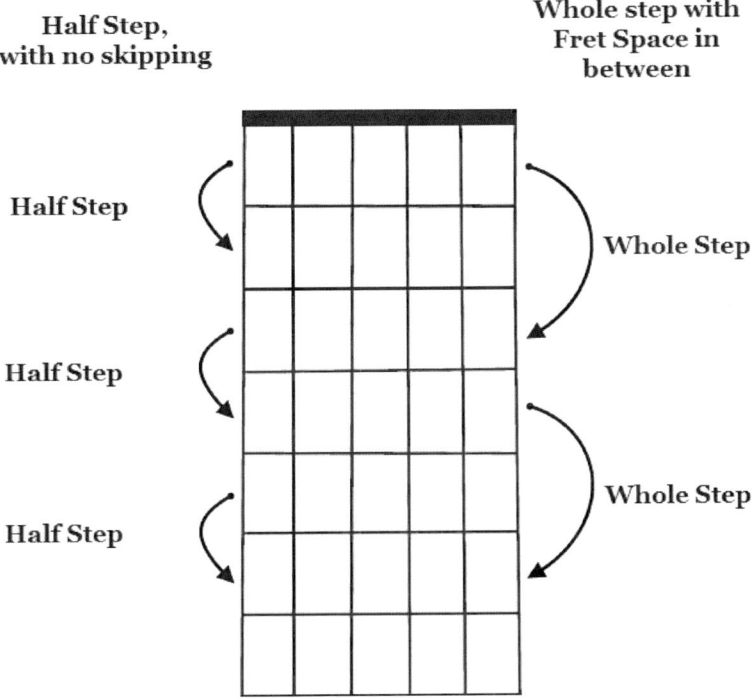

As the diagram above explains, in order to go a half-step versus a whole-step, where a half-step is one fret (skipping over one fret wire), and a whole-step is two frets (skipping two fret wires) you would only skip one fret. So, again, a half-step is one fret (to the next fret) and a whole-step is going two frets (skipping over one fret space in-between.)

What is the alphabet we use in music?
The musical alphabet is a repeated series of seven letters. There are sharps and flats in-between some of them, (which will be explained later,) but we're dealing with the natural alphabet for now. The musical letters are, A, B, C, D, E, F, G, A. Yes, we repeat the A again, and even repeat the entire series of the musical alphabet yet again, such as, A, B, C, D, E, F, G, A, B, C, D, E, F, G, A, B, C, repeating indefinitely.

On a guitar neck, there is usually four octaves on a standard 24-fret guitar. So you'll have to repeat the music alphabet three or more times on the neck of a guitar, depending on the number of frets on your particular guitar. For example, a Fender Strat usually has 22 frets, while an acoustic guitar has a lot less frets, yet both still have over 3 octaves to every scale.

What is an octave?

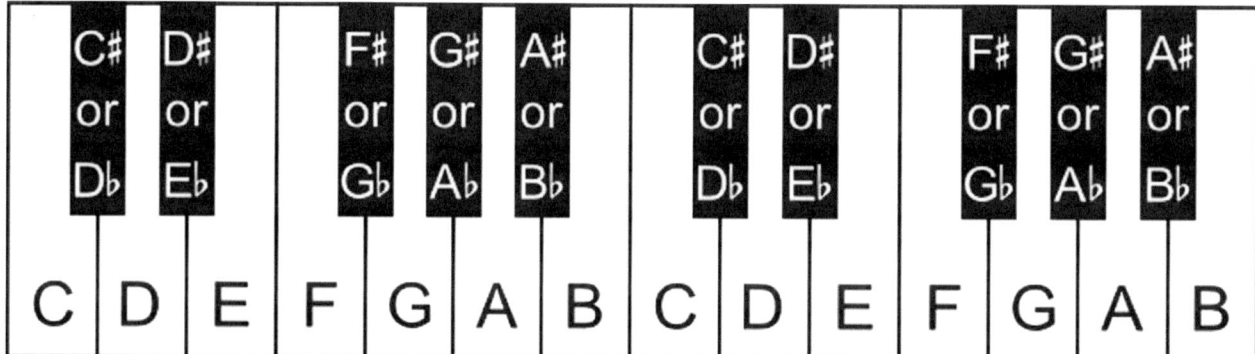

An octave covers from the 1st to the 8th. Every letter will be designated relating to the scale position of 1st, 2nd, 3rd, 4th, 5th, 6th, 7th, and the octave, which is the 8th note in the series. For example, if you start with C in our alphabet, you would move through C, D, E, F, G, A, B, then to the octave C to cover one full octave of the C Major scale. Don't forget, there are sharps and flats between some of these spaces (as shown in the keyboard example, above) but none of the sharp or flat notes are used in the key of C Major, which only uses the natural notes listed above.

What is a sharp and a flat?

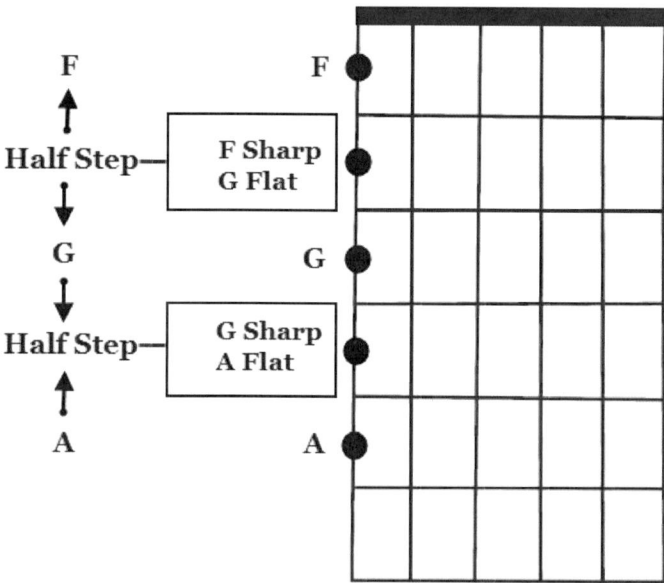

As mentioned before, there are sharps and flats to every note. For example, the A sharp (A♯) or A flat (A♭), both are a half-step in a certain direction from the A note. If you were looking at a note and the natural notes are A, B, C, D, E, F, G, and A, a half-step before A is A♭ toward the G, while a half-step after A is A♯ toward the B.

As well, all sharps and flats have two note names, which can be applied the same note, as follows:

- A♯ is also the exact same note as B♭ .
- C♯ is the exact same note as D♭ .
- D♯ is actually the same exact note as E♭ .
- F♯ is actually the exact same note as G♭ .
- G♯ is actually the same note as A♭ .

These are actually the exact same notes with two different names for the same note. You will notice that I did not mention B♯, C♭ , E♯, or F♭ . Because B and E have no sharps and C and F have no flats. (See the reference.) Though in some music tense, some will say to play a F♭ . This simply is a confusing way to say play an Natural E. Another example is when someone says to play a C♯♯ which again, is a confusing way of saying play a natural D.

What are the normal spaces of a basic melody?

C Major

Do	Re	Mi	Fa	So	La	Ti	Do
1st	2nd	3rd	4th	5th	6th	7th	8th and Octave

The normal spaces of the basic melody are Do-Re-Mi-Fa-So-La-Ti-Do. Where Do is the 1st, or the Root, Re the 2nd, Mi the 3rd, Fa the 4th, So the 5th, La the 6th, Ti the 7th, and Do the octave 8th.

The spaces come from the steps between the basic melody. The 1st (Do), and then a space between to the 2nd (Re), and a space between to the 3rd (Mi) with no space between the 3rd (Mi) and the 4th (Fa), then a space between the 4th (Fa) and the 5th (So), and a space between the 6th (La) and the 7th (Ti), with no space between the 7th (Ti) and the 8th (Do-the octave.) So, this basic patterns is as follows: Do-space-Re-space-Mi-Fa-space-So-space-La-space-Ti-Do. Or, you could say, 1st space, 2nd space, 3rd, 4th space, 5th space, 6th space, 7th, 8th (the octave.)

In essence, when someone says A space B, that space is either an A♯ or a B♭ , which is the same exact note.

Thus ends our preface to Chapter One. I hope I answered enough questions to help guide you through this chapter. If you run across a term in your weekly lessons that confuses you, review this section. Now it's time to start your Guitar Theory Week One.

WEEK ONE: NATURAL NOTES ON THE GUITAR NECK

Week One is an introduction to the key of C Major and the C Major scale. When you were little, you should have learned a very important thing about music in music class, although you probably didn't realize it. It was learning a little song about Do-Re-Mi-Fa-So-La-Ti-Do.

You might say, "What does that have to do with guitar theory?"

Well in short, everything! Scales are based on a simple pattern. That pattern is (I hope you guessed it) the Do-Re-Mi-Fa-So-La-Ti-Do pattern.

Sing it in your head (or aloud) right now. There is a very distinctive pattern to this "simple" pattern. The Do-Re-Mi-Fa-So-La-Ti-Do actually breaks down into whole-step, whole-step, half-step, whole-step, whole-step, whole-step, half-step, which is the basic Major scale pattern. We're going to keep this pattern in the key of C because C has no sharps and no flats.

To further explain this basic Major scale pattern, you'll refer to the diagram below. Starting on C, you will move a whole-step to the second note (D), a whole-step to the third note (E), a half-step to the fourth note (F), a whole-step to the fifth note (G), a whole-step to the sixth note (A), a whole-step to the seventh note (B), and finally a half-step to the eighth or the octave (C).

If you were to look at a piano for a reference, it would be really easy because the black keys are sharps and flats, while the white keys are the natural notes, "natural" meaning not sharp nor flat from the original note.

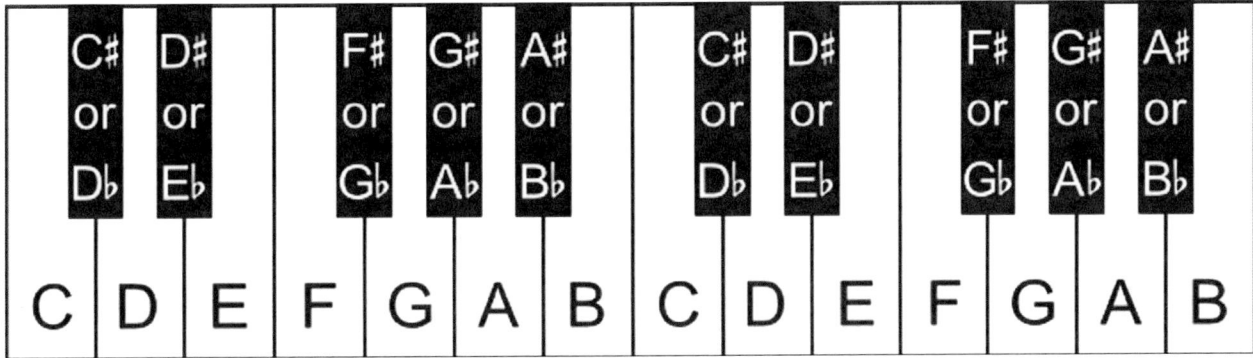

If you start with any C on a piano, and moved up hitting each white key, skipping the black keys you would be playing the Do-Re-Mi-Fa-So-La-Ti-Do pattern just by hitting the eight consecutive notes, as long as you always start at C and end at C. You will notice that the first note and the eighth note are the same, the eighth note being an octave higher, hence the word octave, meaning, "8th."

Now to transpose this to a guitar neck, look at the diagram below:

10 | A Lesson A Week: *The Theory of Guitar Made Easy*

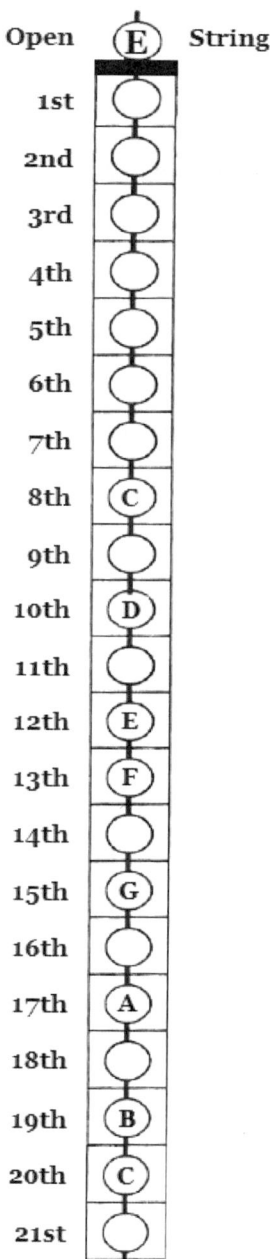

Once you know where the C note is located on your guitar neck, you would follow that up the neck by skipping a whole space, (two frets), to the D. Once you realize that it goes, whole-step, whole-step, half-step, whole-step, whole-step, whole-step, half-step, unlike the piano where you're just skipping the black keys, you'll understand that you're actually skipping a fret space.

Following that logic, you'll go from C to D on the guitar by skipping the fret in between, and from D to E by doing the same. E to F doesn't skip a fret. F to G skips a fret again. G to A would skip a fret again. A to B will skip a fret again. Last but not least, B to C is no skipped fret; it's one after the other. Yes, we go back to the letter C because our musical alphabet is a revolving one that goes C, D, E, F, G, A, B, C. and repeats.

Now you might be confused when hearing terms like whole step, half step, next fret, and skipped fret when referring to a guitar. What does that all mean? Physically, if you start at any fret on the neck and go to the next fret down, for example, from the 4th fret to the 5th fret, "half step or next fret" is exactly what we mean; the next fret down. If you were to go from the 4th fret to the 6th fret instead of the 5th, you would be going a whole-step, or a skipped fret.

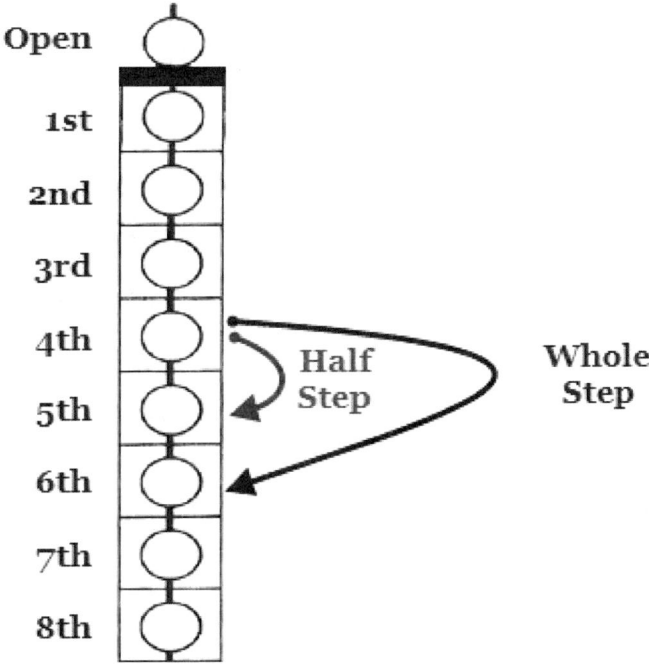

I hope this concept isn't too much for you. Trust me; given time, you will more than understand it. Let's take a second to look at the guitar.

Now let's look at your guitar strings. The guitar has six strings. Starting from the one closest to your eye looking down on your guitar, it is the E string, which is the thickest string. The next is the A string, the D string, the G string, the B string and then the thinnest of all strings is the E string again. Look at the diagram below:

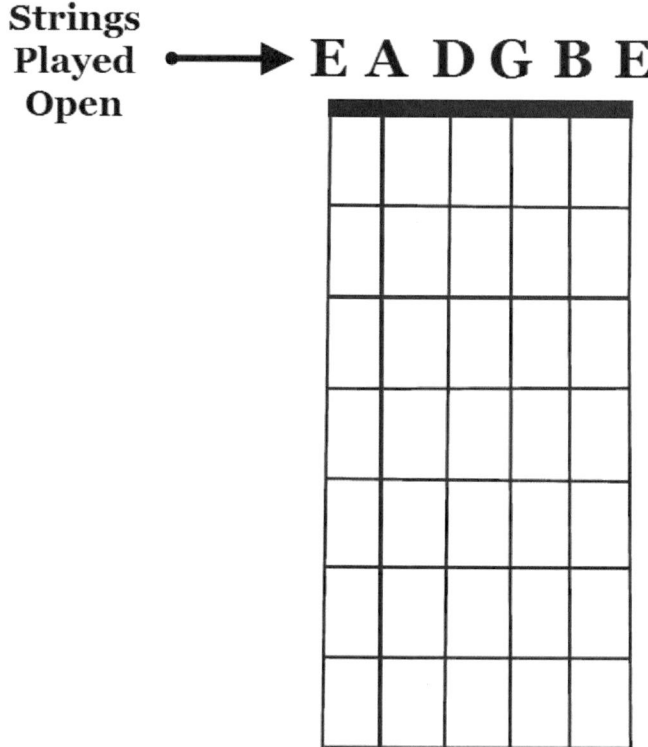

Strings Played Open ⟶ E A D G B E

Every fret down from a particular string you start with as seen in the example, are whole and half-step natural notes that follow the scale pattern that we will also call the, "skip or no skip pattern". Starting with the very top string, which, again, is the thickest string, (the 6th string, the first E string looking down), the note names for the Do-Re-Mi-Fa-So-La-Ti-Do pattern for that E string, are as follows:

- E- the open string.
- F- the very first fret.
- G- skip a fret to reach the G, which is the 3rd fret.
- A- skip a fret to A on the 5th.
- B- skip a fret to B on the 7th.
- C- the next fret (do not skip in-between) to C. Remember, you do not skip fret spaces between B notes and C notes, or E notes and F notes in a C Major scale. All the rest, you skip one full fret to get to the next note that isn't a sharp or a flat, which means you moved on to the 8th fret for the C.
- D- move to the 10th fret down to reach the D.
- E- skip a fret to the 12th fret for the E.
- Continue on the neck, repeating the pattern all over again.

First String Thickest String	Second String	Third String	Fourth String	Fifth String	Sixth String Thinnest String
Open E	Open A	Open D	Open G	Open B	Open E
1st F	1st	1st	1st	1st C	1st F
2nd	2nd B	2nd E	2nd A	2nd	2nd
3rd G	3rd C	3rd F	3rd	3rd D	3rd G
4th	4th	4th	4th B	4th	4th
5th A	5th D	5th G	5th C	5th E	5th A
6th	6th	6th	6th	6th F	6th
7th B	7th E	7th A	7th D	7th	7th B
8th C	8th F	8th	8th	8th G	8th C
9th	9th	9th B	9th E	9th	9th
10th D	10th G	10th C	10th F	10th A	10th D
11th	11th	11th	11th	11th	11th
12th E	12th A	12th D	12th G	12th B	12th E
13th F	13th	13th	13th	13th C	13th F
14th	14th B	14th E	14th A	14th	14th
15th G	15th C	15th F	15th	15th D	15th G
16th	16th	16th	16th B	16th	16th
17th A	17th D	17th G	17th C	17th E	17th A
18th	18th	18th	18th	18th F	18th
19th B	19th E	19th A	19th D	19th	19th B
20th C	20th F	20th	20th	20th G	20th C
21st	21st	21st B	21st E	21st	21st

Refer to the diagram above for the precise frets on each string for the C Major scale. You'll notice that all of the notes on the above diagram are natural notes. They have no sharps and no flats. Once again, they're like the white keys on the piano. So, knowing that same skip or no skip pattern, let's start with the 5th string. The 5th string would be the A string when it's open. So, let's work through the pattern once again:

- Open string is A.
- Placing your finger two frets down on the second fret bracket, skipping the first fret, you are at the B.
- The immediate next fret, you're at the C.
- Skip a fret to reach the D.
- Skip a fret again to the E.
- Now, we don't skip a fret again to reach the F on the 8th fret.
- Skipping a fret down to the 10th fret and you're now at the G.
- Finish by skipping to the 12th fret you're once again back to the A.

What you have so far on two strings is the E played open, first fret F, skip a fret

14 | A Lesson A Week: *The Theory of Guitar Made Easy*

G, skip a fret A, skip a fret B, no skip C, skip a fret D, skip a fret and you've arrived at the 12th fret back to E. Next string is A played open, skip a fret B, don't skip a fret C, skip a fret D, skip a fret E, don't skip a fret F, skip a fret G, skip a fret to the 12th fret back to the A.

You will notice two things:
1. The alphabet keeps repeating itself only with spaces or no spaces in between, so that it goes E, F, G, A, B, C, D, E then it goes A, B, C, D, E, F, G, A.
2. The only thing you really have to pay attention to is that the B and C have no space between them so there is no fret skip. As well, the E and F have no space between them so again no fret skip. All the rest of your notes, A to B, C to D, D to E, F to G, G to A, do have a one space (one fret) between them that you skip to get to the next natural note.

I hope you now know the C Major scale pattern and that you can easily see the examples with the E string and the A string can also be applied to the other four strings. Starting with D, G, B, E, as the open string notes, you should now know when to skip a fret and when not to skip a fret, simply by using the pattern you've learned.

Before moving on, please work through ALL six strings on this pattern starting on E and working down to the next string until you've reached the E again. Attempt each pattern without referring to the diagram above.

Now that you've worked through all six strings by using that pattern, it is time to get into the C Major scale.

Why? Because it has all natural notes. No sharps and no flats. The the pattern you just learned can be started anywhere on the neck of the guitar to give you the C Major scale and its modes. (We'll get more into the modes later.) For example, if you started on the 6th string, the thinnest E string, where is the C note? It is eight frets down. Let's take a look at this exact pattern by referring to the two diagrams below to work out the C Major scale starting on the E string:

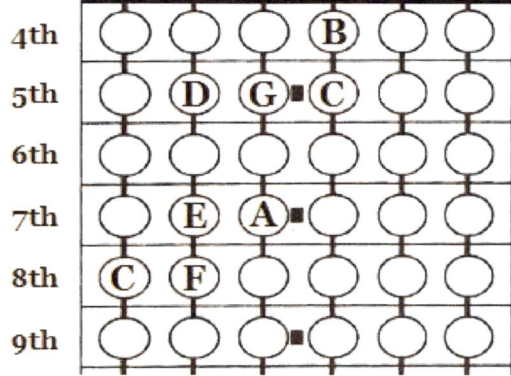
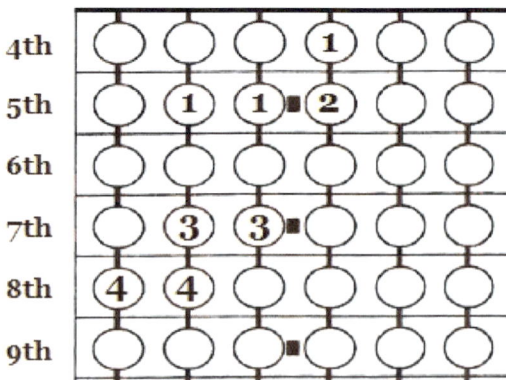

Now that you've studied the diagrams above, let's take a look at each note of the C major scale, starting on the 6th string, on the 8th fret:

- C- 8th fret of the E string using your fourth finger, (pinky).
- D- 5th fret of the next string (A string) with your first finger (pointer finger).
- E- With your 3rd finger, (ring finger) MOVE down two more frets to the 7th fret to hit the E note.
- F- Back to the 8th fret to hit the F with your fourth finger (pinky).
- G- Now, let's move back to the 5th fret on the D string to play the G, with your first finger (pointer).
- A- with your third finger (ring) on the seventh fret, play the A.
- B- Then stretch up to the 4th fret on the G string to play your first finger (pointer) on the B.
- C- last, move down one fret, using your second finger (middle finger) to play the C note on the 5th fret. Remember to refer to the diagram above. You've just played the C Major scale up one octave from C to C.

I'm assuming you've figured out that our second diagram above shows the layout for which finger to use for each fret/note. You need to know that this pattern can be transposed, which is a fancy word for moved up and down the neck of the guitar, string-to-string, as long as you start with the C note, also called the 1st, or the root of the scale. Refer to the diagrams below to understand how this is possible:

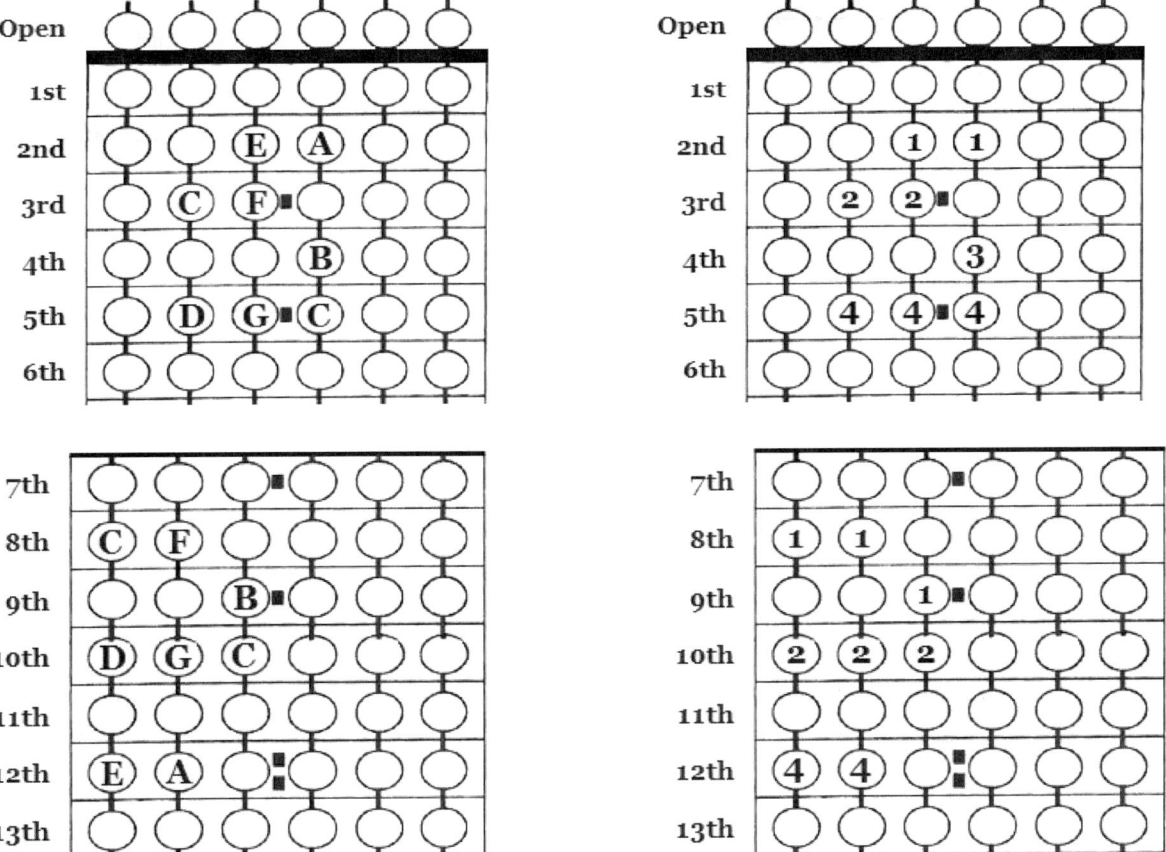

However, please note that the position of the notes and the positioning of your fingers will change with the positioning of where you start, up or down the neck, as long as you start with the C first root-note and end with the octave, and follow the pattern. Let's take a closer look at this pattern. The C Major scale is not as hard as many of the others, because (and I can't say this enough) it has all natural notes. So let's look at the position of the notes in the relative C Major scale:

C Major

C	D	E	F	G	A	B	C
1st (Root)	2nd	3rd	4th	5th	6th	7th	8th (Octave)

The root, also called the 1st note, is the C. The D is the 2nd note of the C Major scale. The E is the 3rd note, also called the third, which is a very important note in the C Major scale. (We'll go into that later when we cover chords in the next chapter.) The F is the 4th. The G is the 5th (the fifth,) which is another important note when talking about chord structures with scales. The A is the 6th. The B is the 7th. The last note is back to the C as its octave, or 8th note, which will be eight full notes (octave) higher than the original C you played.

There is a standard of four octaves on a 24-fret guitar. From E string to E string is two octaves across. So. there should be a two octave pitch difference from your 6th, or low E string (thickest), to your 1st, or bottom E string (thinnest). Refer to the diagram below to understand where these octaves fall on the neck of the guitar:

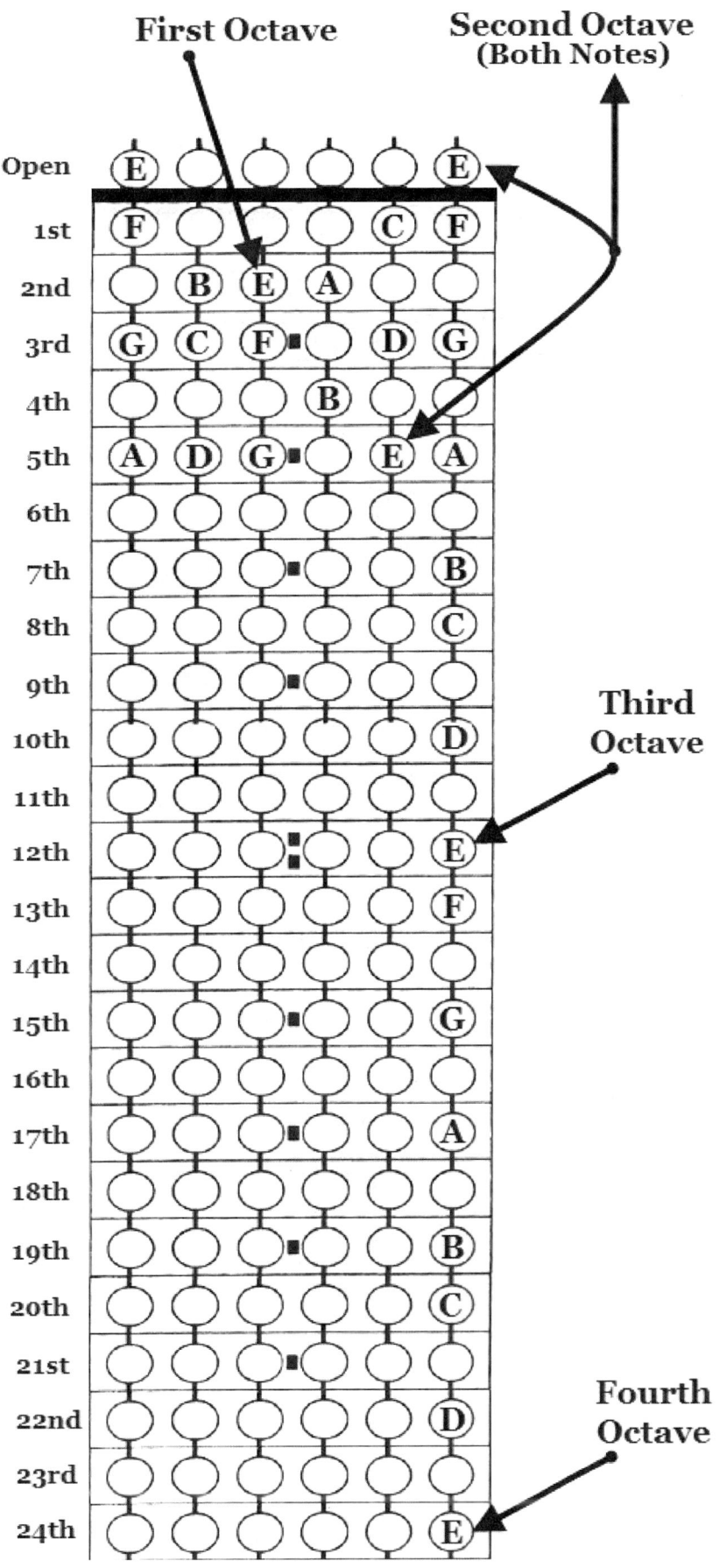

The next example (see the diagram below) is of another C Major scale and all the positions on the neck of the guitar. You can start at any C and go up one octave. (Starting at C and stopping at the octave C.)

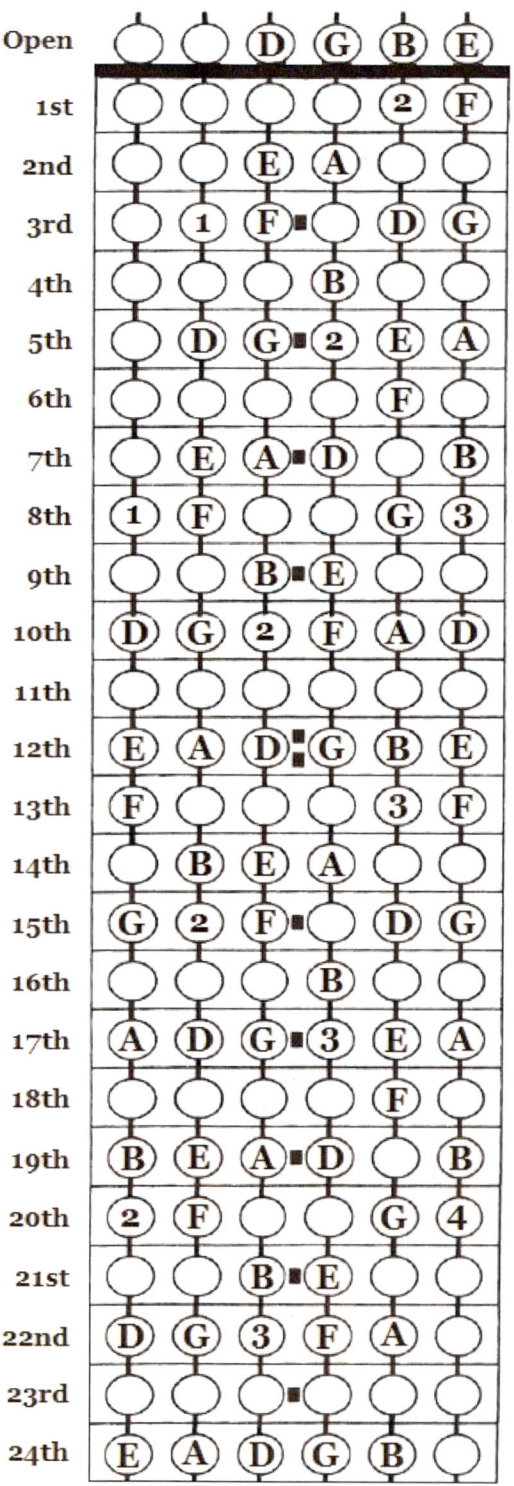

Play ANY Pattern of the C Major Scale

C to C
1 to 2
2 to 3
3 to 4

Please remember, a Major scale is not a solo. It is a tool used for soloing around the major scale. I'm hoping this will help you with the theory behind scalular playing, and help you to incorporate them into your solos.

This concludes Week One. Study this lesson every day for one full week before moving on to Week Two.

WEEK TWO: BASIC CHORDS IN C MAJOR

This week, we begin breaking down how chords are made from the scales and how they are to be used in Major, Minor, and Diminished modes. To create a basic chord, you would take the first, third, and fifth (1st, 3rd, and 5th) out of a major scale to create a chord. For example, if you played the first, third, and fifth (or the the C, E, and G notes) of the C Major scale, you would have the C Major Chord. Please note that in this example, the C, E, and G notes are all in their natural positions, which make the C Major chord.

To understand the relationship between all the chords that fit into a C Major scale, we must do a quick run-through of the other note name scales to understand how we can fit certain chords into the C Major scale. Let's now look at each scale below:

D Major Scale

The D Major scale has two sharps. In our next chapter, we're going into the circle of fifths, which will better guide you to remember the sharps/flats. For now, let's stick with this simple explanation of the D Major scale. As mentioned, unlike the C Major scale, the D Major scale has two sharps and consists of D, E, F♯, G, A, B, C♯, back to D. If we look at that D chord, as applied to a C Major scale, we can't take the natural 1st, natural 3rd, and natural 5th from the D major scale. Why? Because the F♯ will not fit into the C Major. So we flatten the third to the F natural note, which creates a D Minor chord to fit into a C Major scale. To "flatten" a note means to go a half-step, or a fret space, in one direction. In this case, to flatten the note means to go a half step lower, from F♯ down to F. To sharpen a note means to go a half-step higher, for example, from F up to F♯.

E Major Scale

The E Major scale has four sharps and consists of E, F♯, G♯, A, B, C♯, D♯, back to E. You will notice that the third is a G♯, which again needs to be flattened for the C Major scale. You will also notice that every scale still follows the same alphabet pattern, from first-to-octave, one letter each, though we are now adding a sharp to a few of the letters. Since the third, or, 3rd, is G♯, we need to flatten it to G in order to fit this chord into the C Major scale to create the E,G,B chord, which creates an E Minor chord.

Note: Going forward in the book, when referring to note positions, such as a "third", please note that it is acceptable to replace the spelling of third with 3rd, as they both refer to the same position.

F Major Scale

The F Major scale may seem problematic to you at first because it has no sharps. Instead, it has one flat, which is the fret before (or the space before) the actual natural note. So, the F Major scale has one flat and consists of F, G, A, B♭, C, D, E, back to F. Notice that the first, third, and fifth are all natural notes, which means the F Major chord fits perfectly into the C Major scale.

G Major Scale
The G Major scale has one sharp and consists of G, A, B, C, D, E, F♯, back to G. You'll notice that the first, third, and fifth are all naturals, which means there is no need to modify the G chord to fit into the C Major scale because a G major chord consists of G, B, and D.

A Major Scale
The A Major scale has three sharps and consists of A, B, C♯, D, E, F♯, G♯, back to A. So, again we need to flatten the 3rd, which results in an A Minor chord that fits perfectly into a C Major scale.

B Major Scale
The B Major scale has five sharps, which consists of B, C♯, D♯, E, F♯, G♯, A♯, back to B. Notice only the B and E in the B Major scale are the only natural notes. The rest are all sharps. To transpose this over to a chord that would fit into the C Major scale, you have to flatten both the 3rd and the 5th creating what is called a *Diminished* chord. The difference between a Diminished chord and a Minor chord is that the 5th is also flattened, along with the 3rd in a Diminished chord. In this case the D♯ and the F♯ both have to be flattened to D and F to fit into the scale of C Major. These patterns hold true for all the different scales.

Always remember to look both at the scale you are playing in compared to the other scales for a clue. As in our examples above, you'll recall that when playing in a C Major scale, the D chord could not stay major when used in the C Major scale because the 3rd in the D Major scale is an F♯. Since a C Major scale contains no sharps, the F♯ needs to be flattened F in order to fit in with the C Major scale.

Now it's time for a trick question to test what you've learned to far...Does the F note fit into the C Major scale? Knowing all the notes in the C Major scale, does the F♯ fit in, which is a half-step above the F? One fits; one doesn't. You should know the answer.

Let's look at all the notes of each chord in a C Major scale as-is without the concept of scales, C E G, D F A, E G B, F A C, G B D, A C E, and B D F. Again we see all natural notes, with no sharps or flats. Hence, by just looking at the chords we can see the scale they belong to, which in this case, is C Major. We will also learn what other keys can be thrown in to add flavor when we learn which notes to stay away from, or more precisely, which chords to avoid. (But that is for a later chapter.)

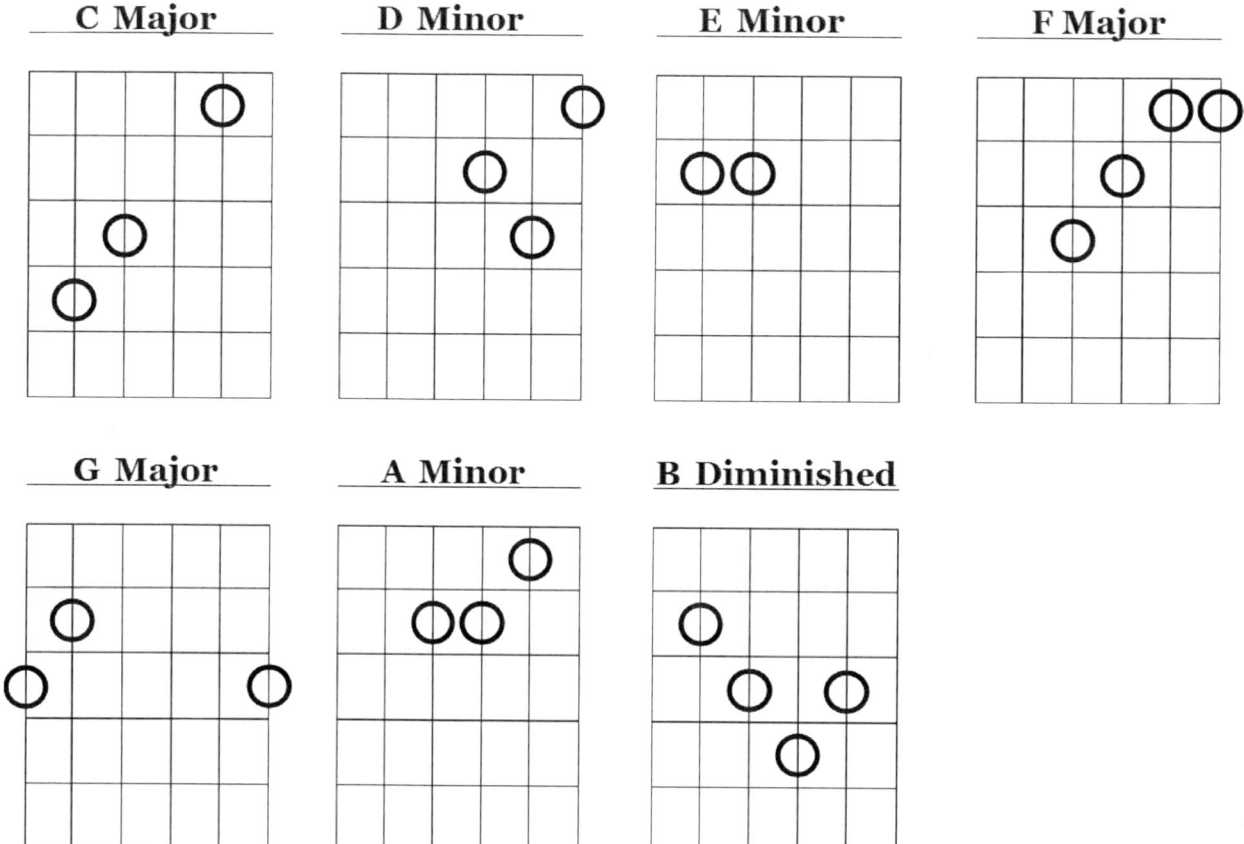

So, for a quick reference of chords to play with the C Major scale, (or any Major scale just transposing the notes to fit with any proper scale or mode,) please refer to the diagrams above.

In the diagrams above, we have the following chords:
- **C Major** taken from the C Major scale with a Natural 1st, Natural 3rd, and the Natural 5th.
- **D Minor** taken from the D Major scale, with a Natural 1st, Flatted 3rd, and Natural 5th.
- **E Minor** taken from the E Major scale, with Natural 1st, Flatted 3rd, and Natural 5th.
- **F Major** taken from the F Major scale, with a Natural 1st, Natural 3rd, and Natural 5th.
- **G Major** taken from the G Major scale with a Natural 1st, Natural 3rd, and Natural 5th.
- **A Minor**, or a Natural Minor, taken from the A Major scale with a Natural 1st, a flattened 3rd, and a Natural 5th.
- **B Diminished** which is the unique chord we mentioned earlier in this lesson, with its flattened 3rd and flattened 5th. This is a chord you will never want to end a progression on, for it will leave the progression sounding unresolved.

Now, let's take a look at another basic chord pattern, such as the 1, 4, 5. The 1, 4, 5 pattern is just what it says; the first chord, the fourth chord, and the fifth chord of a scale. In our example, it is the C, F, G, taken from the C Major scale as the first note transposed into a chord, as well as the the fourth note and the fifth note transposed into chords, which, again, is the C, F, and G. In a C Major scale, all three of our chords are Major by looking at their individual scales, because their 1st, 3rd, and 5th are all natural notes. So, this gives us C Major, F Major, and G Major.

Now note, all of the chords in the C Major scale would actually be as follows: C Major, D Minor, E Minor, F Major, G Major, A Minor, and B Diminished. All of these chords can be used if you're playing a chord progression in the key of C Major. I do not mean to sound like a broken record by repeating myself, but it is the only way to help you commit guitar theory to memory. Repetition makes permanent, so you will be asked to repeatedly read each section and practice what you've learned repeatedly, as well as notice that I repeat myself quite often. This is on purpose because I am determined to help you succeed!

Before moving on to Week Three, please study and learn the chords for the C Major scale on your guitar and refer to the other scales to see how each chord in a C Major scale, such as the E Minor, is altered from the original E Major scale. As a final guide, refer to the diagram below to recall how many sharps or flats are present in each Major scale.

Study hard and I will see you in a week!

SCALE:

C Major No #s, No ♭s	C		D		E	F		G		A		B
D Major 2 #s	D		E		F#	G		A		B		C#
E Major 4 #s	E		F#		G#	A		B		C#		D#
F Major 1 ♭	F		G		A	B♭		C		D		E
G Major 1 #	G		A		B	C		D		E		F#
A Major 3 #s	A		B		C#	D		E		F#		G#
B Major 5 #s	B		C#		D#	E		F#		G#		A#

WEEK THREE: MODES OF THE C MAJOR SCALE

This week, we're going to go through the basic modes and explain their positioning in correlation to the C Major scale, which refer to the seven modes of the C Major scale.

Ionian →	C		D		E	F		G		A		B	C
Dorian →	D		E	F		G		A		B	C		D
Phrygian →	E	F		G		A		B	C		D		E
Lydian →	F		G		A		B	C		D		E	F
Mixolydian →	G		A		B	C		D		E	F		G
Aeolian →	A		B	C		D		E	F		G		A
Locrian →	B	C		D		E	F		G		A		B

First, let's review the C Major scale on the diagram above as applied to the seven modes. A mode is simply starting a scale in a different position other than the first. Once you've studied the diagram, let's review each mode:

Ionian Mode
The very first position with a Major scale is known as the Ionian mode. In this mode, C Major it starts with the C and goes through the octave of C, hence, C, D, E, F, G, A, B, C.

Dorian Mode
The second mode of the C Major scale, or any scale, is the Dorian mode. It is called the D Dorian in the C Major scale, being that the D is the second note of the C Major scale. You always start with the second note of any scale to create the Dorian mode. If you wanted to look at just the Dorian mode in steps, it would be 1st, step, 2nd, 3rd, step, 4th, step, 5th, step, 6th, 7th, step to the octave.

Don't let this confuse you. It's just the same as the Major Do-Re-Mi scale, starting in the second position, which is Re. In the case of the C Major scale, Dorian mode starts on the D note, hence, D, E, F, G, A, B, C, octave D.

The flavor of the Dorian mode is Minor. What does that mean? When we examined chords in our previous weekly lesson, we noticed that some chords are Major, some chords are Minor, and some chords are Diminished. This is the same for the modes, as they are all Major or Minor, and in one case Diminished. To correlate along with these same patterns, let's continue through the rest of the modes.

Phrygian Mode
The Third mode, the Phrygian Mode, is another Minor mode. A mode is useful when we use Majors and Minors because they do something that's called a *strain*,

which is a difference in tonal value that sets a mood. The third of the C Major scale is the E Phrygian. It will start with the E note and follow the same note pattern based on the C Major, which was also followed by the D (Dorian or Minor mode). This means we will move from E to an octave of E with no sharps or flats, or simply, E, F, G, A, B, C, D, octave E. In steps, this would be 1st, 2nd, step, 3rd, step, 4th, step, 5th, 6th, step, 7th, step, octave.

Time for a quick refresher. What are steps? They're your fingering placements on the neck. When there is no-step, you're not going to skip a fret. You're going to go to the immediate next fret. When I say *step* or *skip*, you are going to skip a fret in-between your current fret to the fret that is two frets down. In other words, there will be a fret in-between, which is a skipped fret or a step. If we say step or no-step, or skip or no-skip, remember that we are simply referring to the distance from one fret to another. Let's move onto the next mode.

Lydian Mode
Our fourth mode is the Lydian mode, which is a Major mode. What makes this a Major mode versus a Minor mode is that the third note is always natural or flattened from the original position. All we need to know is that the first, third, and fifth of this scale are in Major note mode, which means they are naturals. In the C Major scale, the Lydian Mode starts on F. As usual it will go from F to octave F, or simply, F, G, A, B, C, D, E, octave F, or, 1st, skip, 2nd, skip, 3rd, skip, 4th, 5th, skip, 6th, skip, 7th, the octave.

This skip, no-skip pattern will remain the same for all of the Lydian modes for any scale you wish to transpose to, whether transposing from C to D, C to G, etc. Memorizing these patterns will give you a vast pool of Lydian mode playing, or any mode playing for the matter. Again, remember that I've only chosen to focus on the C Major modes to make it relatively easy, BUT, you'll soon learn that it is relatively simple to transpose to ANY key. The easy way to look at it why we are using C Major as our focal point is to look as a piano keyboard. On a keyboard, any modes based on the key of C Major would mean that you'd only have to play the white keys and none of the black keys in-between, because there are no sharps or flats. Now, let's look at the Mixolydian mode.

Mixolydian Mode
The Mixolydian mode is the rock-n-roll standard guitar player mode. A lot of guitar players use the Mixolydian mode as the go-to mode for rock-n-roll playing. This mode is not to be confused with Blues Rock or Pentatonic Rock, which is covered in Chapter Four,. However, you'll soon learn that the Mixolydian even fits in there too and can be used to your advantage once you have a grasp on guitar theory. In the C Major scale, the mode would be the G Mixolydian mode, which is a Major mode, going from G to octave G, or, G, A, B, C, D, E, F, octave G. On your guitar fretboard, that means the Mixolydian will be G, skip, A, skip, B, C, skip, D, skip, E, F, skip, octave G. So again, 1st note, skip, 2nd, skip, 3rd, 4th, skip, 5th, skip, 6th, 7th, skip, and octave. Now, it's time for another Minor mode.

Aeolian Mode

Hey, we've only got only two modes to go! The sixth mode is the Minor Aeolian, which is the Natural Minor. You will hear that alot; Natural Minor. The sixth Natural Minor Aeolian is of course A. We'll go from A to octave A, or, A, B, C, D, E, F, G, octave A. Step-wise, the pattern will go, 1st, skip, 2nd, 3rd, skip, 4th, skip, 5th, 6th, skip, 7th, skip, octave.

I hope by now we have impressed upon you that every note has a skip-space or a skip-fret, between C to D, D to E, F to G, G to A, and A to B, and no skipped space, AKA no skipped fret between B to C and E to F. This also works the same backwards; D to C, E to D, G to F, A to G, and B to A and the same with no skip from C to B and F to E. If you review the modes we've already covered, you'll start to make this relationship. Let's move on to our last mode for this lesson.

Locrian Mode

The seventh and last mode of the C Major scale is the Diminished Locrian mode. In the key of C Major, it is B Locrian. As the modes before, you're going octave to octave, or B to octave B. The notes are B, C, D, E, F, G, A, octave B, or, 1st, 2nd, skip, 3rd, skip, 4th, 5th, skip, 6th, skip, 7th, and skip, octave. The reason it's called the Diminished Locrian (not to be confused with the actual Diminished scale) is that both the third and fifth notes are flattened from their original position in the original Major scale. A Diminished Locrian is more than just a Minor version scale, such as the Aeolian or the Dorian, because of the flatted 5th. Actually, it would be proper to call the Locrian scale, Diminished.

Now that you understand the modes, let's move on to review the notes on the guitar neck. On the position of the neck, it comes into play that every single fret will be a note, either natural or sharp/flat. Refer to the diagram below:

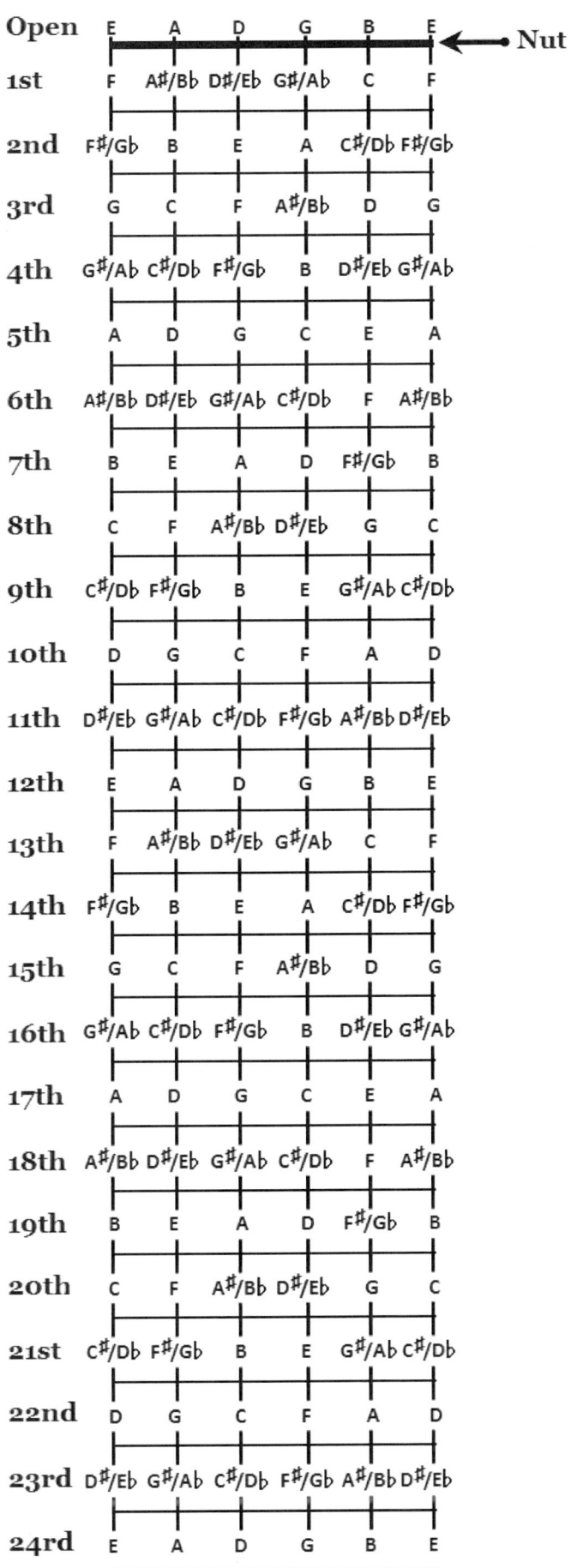

28 | A Lesson A Week: *The Theory of Guitar Made Easy*

As you study the diagram above, look at the open E string. When the string is played open, it is an E. But, once your finger touches the fret, the notes will change. For example, when placing your finger on the the first note on the 1st fret, you'll notice that is changes to an F. The second note is an F♯ on the 2nd fret. The note of the 3rd fret is a G. The next fret is a G♯. The 5th fret down will of course by an A. The next fret down is the A♯. The 7th fret is a B. The 8th fret is a C. The 9th fret is a C♯. The 10th fret is a D. The 11th fret is a D♯. That will bring us back to an octave of the open E on the 12th fret.

"Wait a second! Did I hear that right? There's an open note AND twelve frets to the octave? There are thirteen notes all together?"

You heard correct. Let me explain. Starting with the C Major scale, we would have, as we've gone over already, the 1st root note C. The space note C♯. The 2nd note of the C Major scale, the D. The next note space of D♯. The 3rd note of the C Major scale, the E. The non-skip note right to the 4th note of the C Major scale, which is the F. The next skipped note of F♯. The 5th note of the C Major scale, the G. The next skipped space of G♯. The next 6th note of the C Major scale, the A. The next skipped space the A♯. The next 7th note of the C Major scale, the B. The next non-skipped space is the octave C.

So, the C Major scale is skipping those notes. C♯, D♯, F♯, G♯, and A♯. They are still notes that exist, only they do not fit into the Natural C Major scale, which is why you skip them. So in truth, we have thirteen notes in total on the neck of the guitar and the scales are those notes we play where we skip or don't skip frets to miss notes that do not fit into our scale. These scales, modes, and even chords that we're now getting into can be played in any position on the neck if you follow the skip and no-skip patterns.

These scales, modes, and chords can be transposed anywhere on the neck if you start with the starting notes, and keep the notes the same. They can be transposed anywhere on the neck like in the following diagram examples:

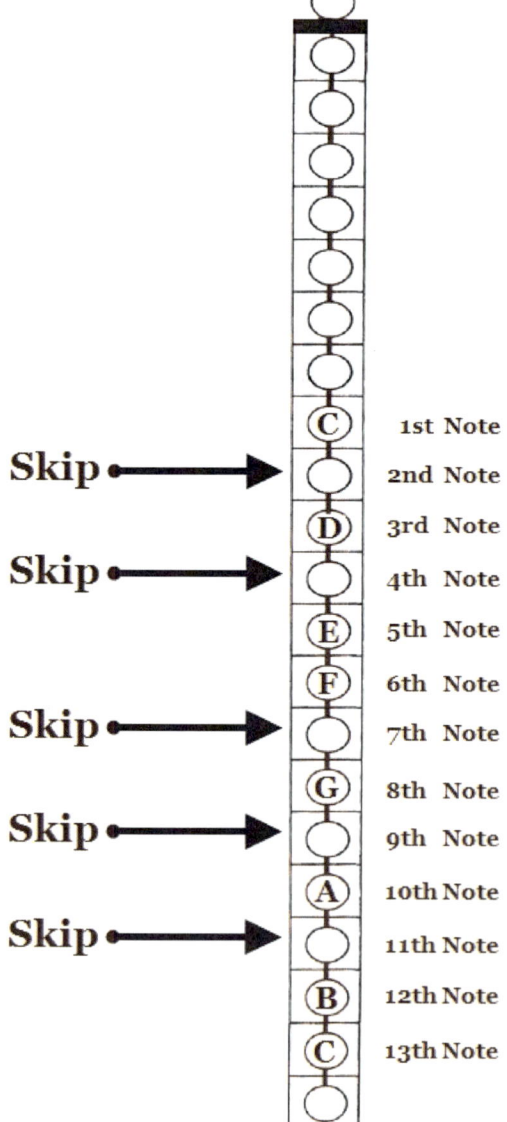

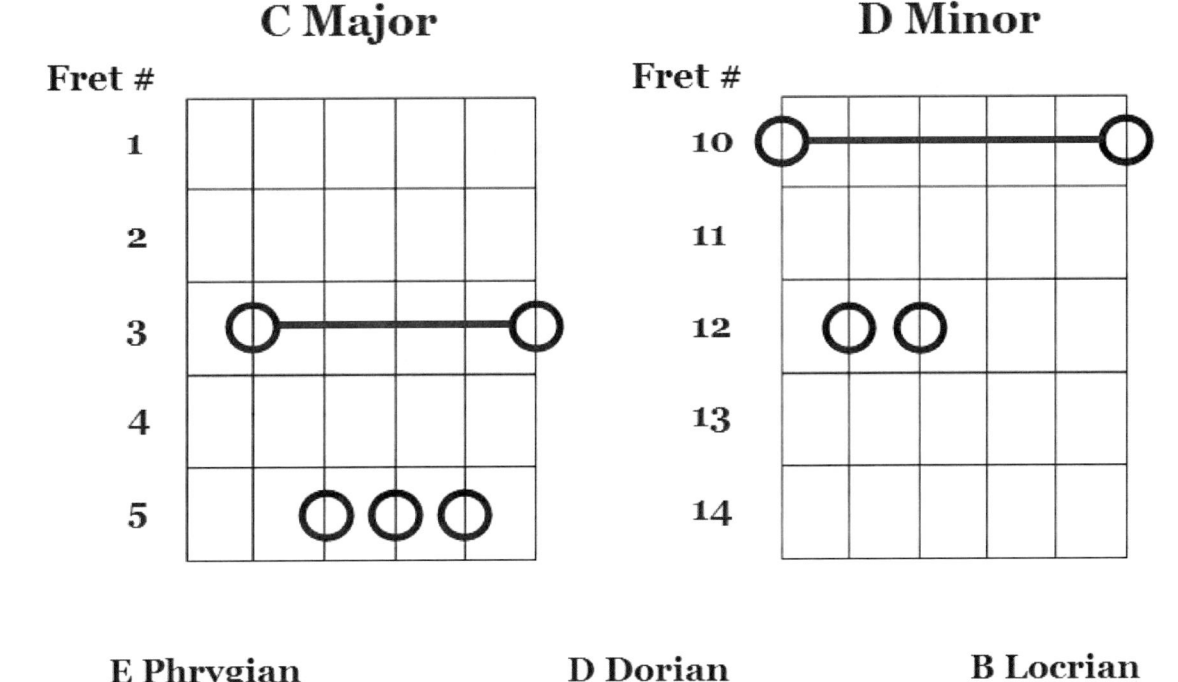

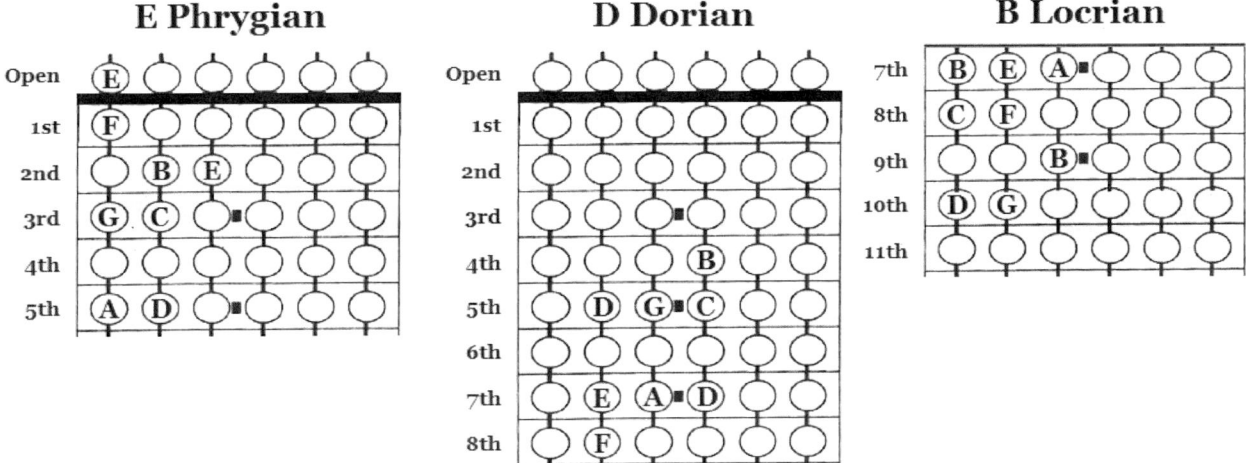

If any of this confuses you, simply read it over again, paying particular attention to the patterns. Remember, you have a full week to study this lesson. Once you learn a pattern for the C Major scale, the easiest thing will be to bring it down a whole-step to the D, and then starting with the D note, playing the exact same pattern; you are now playing the D Major scale.

It really is that easy. You learn one pattern for the C Major scale on the neck, starting at the C Natural note. Next, you move down one full position to the D Natural note and play the exact same pattern. This can be done for EVERY Major scale, no matter the sharps or flats, simply by starting on any note, for example, the E, and using the exact same pattern that you used for C Major. This applies to the F, the G...all of them.

So once you learn the patterns of scales and modes for the key of C Major, you just transpose it to the key you wish to now be in. If you're in C Major, you play a pattern. Now, you wish to play in E Major, so you play that same pattern by starting on the Natural note E, four frets down.

In truth, the key to all this (now that you understand scales, chords, and modes a bit better) is the patterns and the importance of the starting note. I hope you are enjoying reading this book as much as I've enjoyed writing it and if you learned something, even better. Study hard this week, working through all the modes for the C Major scale, (even if you haven't tackled transposing to other keys yet) because your first review is coming up in seven days!

WEEK FOUR: REVIEW

By now, you should have a grasp of the natural notes on the neck of your guitar, and how they relate to the C Major scale and all of the modes. You should look over those modes and practice playing them daily. You should know the chords that follow the progression of the C Major scale and even practice playing the mode that would go with each of those chords. For example, the D Dorian over the D Minor chord, the G Mixolydian over the G Major. etc.

If you have any questions on where what should go, look back into what you studied. First go to the basics of Chapter One, playing a 1-4-5 (C Major/F Major/G Major) progression slowly, and playing the mode to each as you progress. Remember that the 1-4-5 progression does not have to be in order. You could do a G-C-F progression, just to stay in the mode that goes with the chord.

Before moving on to Chapter Two, study this entire chapter until you can answer the questions below so that you have a solid understanding of the C Major scale and the corresponding chords and modes of the C Major scale. Make sure you can answer the following questions before moving on:

- What are the open string notes on the neck of the guitar?
- What are the natural notes on the neck of the guitar?
- What is the difference between a whole-step and a half-step on the neck of the guitar?
- What is the difference between a whole-step and half-step in scale theory?
- What notes make up a chord?
- Where are the C Major scales and notes on the neck of the guitar?
- What note does each of the modes start with in the C Major scale?
- What positioning does each of the modes start with?
- What chords go with the C Major scale?
- What modes correspond with the C Major scale?
- What does the Do-Re-Mi pattern have to do with the Major scales?
- How do you transpose the C Major scale up an octave or two on the neck of the guitar?
- Which notes have Sharps and Flats, and which don't?
- Which sharps and flats are the exact same note?
- How do you play the different modes on the neck of the guitar?

Study hard this week and make sure you know all the material from the first chapter before moving on to Chapter Two.

CHAPTER TWO: AN IN-DEPTH STUDY OF CHORDS

In Chapter Two, you will advance into the world of guitar theory. Remember, the goal is to enhance your playing, while helping you understand the theory behind what you are playing. Hopefully, this knowledge will help you in your musical endeavor. Before we begin studying, let's cover a basic breakdown of each week from Chapter Two, as well as cover a basic explanation of terms you will encounter, such as, "arpeggio" and "power chord" before beginning our new studies:

Week Five: An Introduction to Power Chords
In Week Five, we will cover a basic explanation of power chords, the suspended third, and playing and uses.

Week Six: An Introduction to Arpeggios in the C Major scale
Week Six focuses on an explanation of the broken chord and scalular playing of arpeggios.

Week Seven: The Circle of Fifths
The Circle of Fifths is explained in Week Seven, which is a very important pool of information to help you master the Major and Minor Chords and progressions.

Week Eight: Review
During the final week of this Chapter Two, you will review what you've learned from the previous weeks of this book.

Before We Get Started
Here is your quick preface to questions that might arise during the reading of this chapter.

What does it mean to suspend a chord?
To suspend a chord means to remove the 3rd of the chord and replace it with the 2nd, 4th, or nothing at all. Removing the 3rd frees up a chord to be played with both Major or Minor scales and modes, and can also add different tonal flavors by adding additional scales for different voicings.

What is a power chord?
A power chord is a regular Major or Minor chord where you suspend the 3rd.
To suspend the 3rd, you simply play either another note (the 2nd or 4th) in place of the 3rd, or, as in most power chords, you just remove it. You will play the very first note, which is the root note, and the 5th. This is sometimes called, "Playing the 5ths" or "Playing a 5th chord," if you don't add the 2nd or 4th. Power chords are valuable to playing Rock and Metal because removing the 3rd gives you the advantage of not having a chord that is Major or Minor.

What is a suspended 5th?
A suspended 5th is a fancy way of saying the root and 5th, aka a power chord, (see above). Again, it is simply removing the 3rd from the basic chord.

What is a chromatic?
A chromatic means to play each note ONLY a half step away from each other, so literally one after the other, as in, C, C♯, D, D♯, E etc. A chromatic scale would be exactly that, every note played a half step, with no skips.

What does it mean to augment a note?
To augment a note means to sharpen a note that usually wouldn't be sharp, (raising a half step). For example, to play a chord with an Augmented 5th, you simply sharpen the 5th a half step.

What is an arpeggio?
Arpeggio literally means, "broken chord." It is a chord that is played one note at a time, sometimes sweep picking, (or sweeping) or sometimes just in a melodic tempo, but never strummed like a normal chord.

What is sweep picking (or sweeping)?
Sweep picking is a style where you brush across the strings quickly or alternate picking, but extremely fast. It is not so fast as to be considered a strum, but in such a way that each individual note can be heard and distinguished.

What is the Circle of Fifths?
The Circle of Fifths is a circular chart based on Major scales, designed to signify the sharps and flats of each scale. Starting from C Major, which has no sharps or flats, moving around in a circle to the right (clockwise) with each scale gaining a sharp or flat.

What is the Circle of Fourths?
The Circle of Fourths is the exact same as the Circle of Fifths, but going around the Circle to the left (counter-clockwise) instead of the right (clockwise) losing sharps or flats with every descending key, as it returns to the key of C Major, which has no sharps or flats

What is chugging?
Chugging, or the "chugging method," is repetitive strumming, sometimes in one direction, with two or more strums per second.

What is tonality?
Tonality is the relationship between the notes of the scale or key.

What is a bar chord?
When you bar a finger fully across a fret on the neck of the guitar, and use your other fingers to make the rest of the chord, you are creating a bar chord.

What are ♯ and ♭ symbols?
These are the musical symbols for Sharp (♯) and Flat (♭).

    Thus ends our preface of Chapter Two. Now it's time to start your Guitar Theory Week Five.

WEEK FIVE: AN INTRODUCTION TO POWER CHORDS

A power chord is just a fancy name for chords that contain no thirds. Take a look at the diagrams below to better understand:

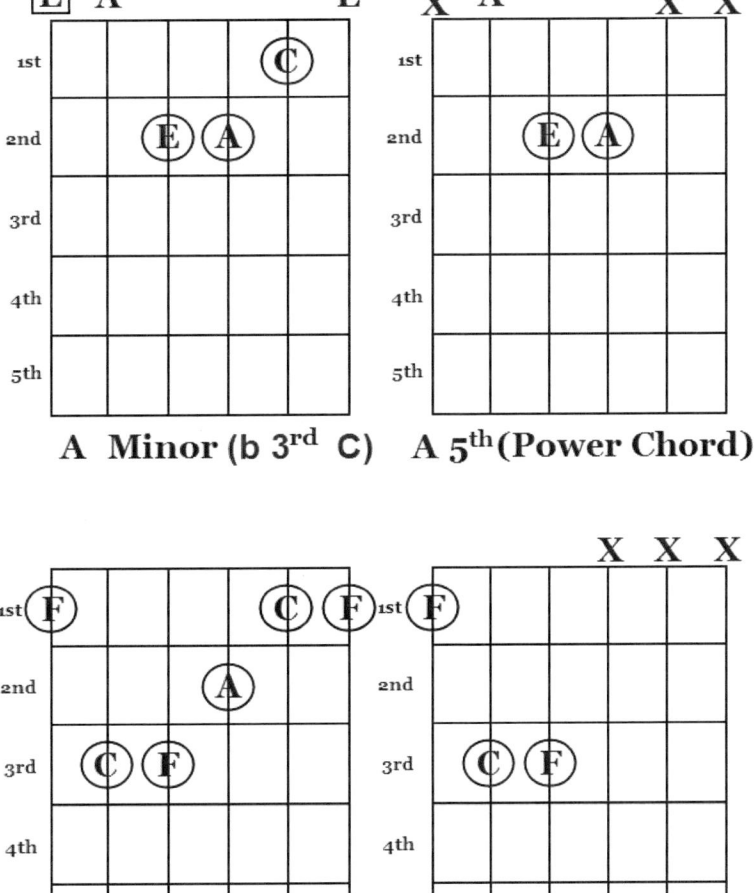

The benefit to playing a bar chord is that you don't have to worry about Majors and Minors, because they lack the 3rd to color the chord. In some cases, you might even replace the 3rd with a 2nd or a 4th. The 2nd is a full step down from the natural 3rd, which is also a half step down from the Minor flatted 3rd. In the case of a suspended 4th, you will raise the natural 3rd up a half step, or a full step for the Minor flatted 3rd.

In both cases, you are removing the 3rd to add in a new note. For those of you who already have an understanding of some of these concepts, this is not to be confused with 9th chords or 11th chords, which add in the 2nd and 4th, which are the same notes, only in the 9th and 11th positions. In other words, these are the exact same notes, only an octave higher, just like the octave 8th is the same note as the root 1st.

I need you to understand that with the guitar, unlike the piano, the octave higher 9th and 11th does not actually have to be in the octave higher position………WHAT?????

Unlike scales, when creating chords, the actual positions of being placed a full octave higher doesn't matter for chord positionings. I know that it might sound a little difficult, but try to understand, you are limited by finger placements with chords to be able to "voice" these chords. If you actually added the 9th or 11th in the octave above the 2nd and 4th placements, you might, in some cases, need to add fingers to your hands.

So, what is the real difference between a 2nd chord and a 9th, or a 4th chord and an 11th? The 2nd and 4th are suspended (no 3rd) and the 9th and 11th chords have a 3rd and are Major or Minor (natural 3rd or flatted 3rd). So, if a chord has the note and no 3rd, it is the suspended (3rd or 4th). But if it has the 3rd (natural or flatted) then it is the other version of the chord (the 9th or 11th).

Now back to power chords, aka 5th chords, Unlike the suspended 2nd or suspended 4th, the power chord does not add a new note. It just removes the 3rd, and is played by only voicing or playing the 1st (root) and the 5th, with no 3rd or added note at all.

By removing the 3rd, added scale patterns will actually work now, but you'll still have to follow the basic pattern to the scale that you were using. We've learned that the C Major scale follows a pattern of chords that are, C Major, D Minor, E Minor, F Major, G Major, A Minor, and B Diminished. The beauty of power chords is that you don't have to do all that. By suspending the 3rd in our chords, we take away the need for Majors and Minors. (In the case of the B diminished though, we will still need to flatten the 5th.) Look at the examples in the diagrams below to understand the difference between an actual chord and a power chord:

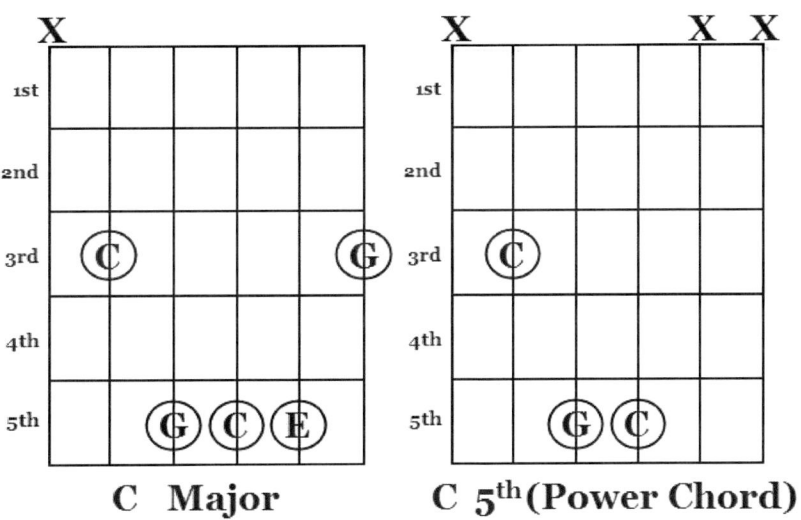

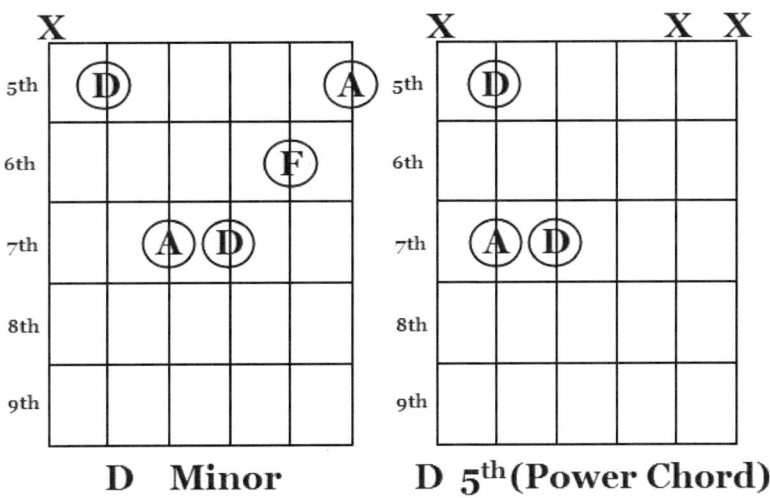

38 | A Lesson A Week: *The Theory of Guitar Made Easy*

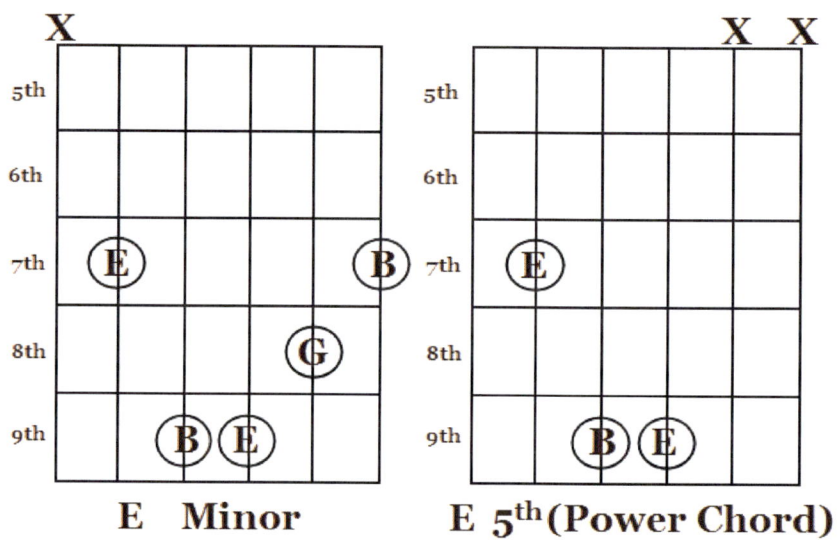

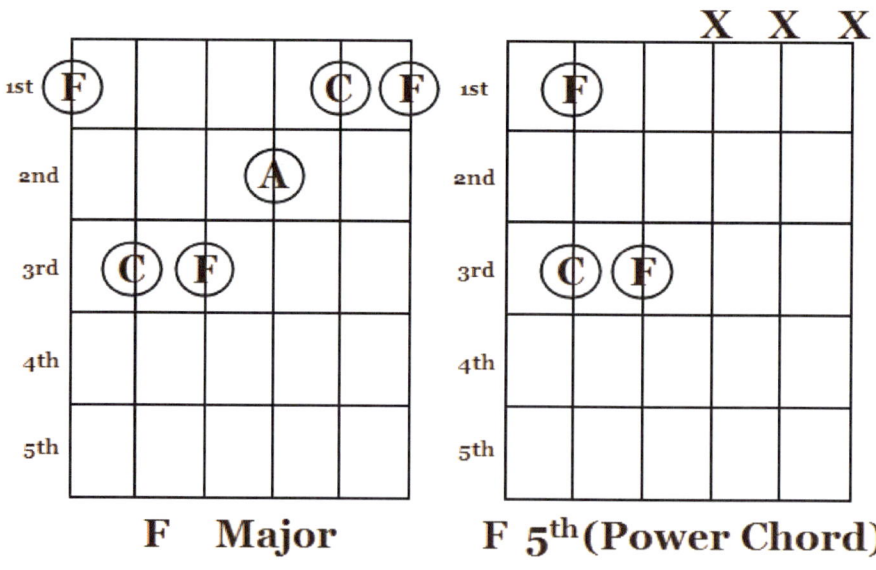

**X = Mute to Deaden,
or Try Not to Play**

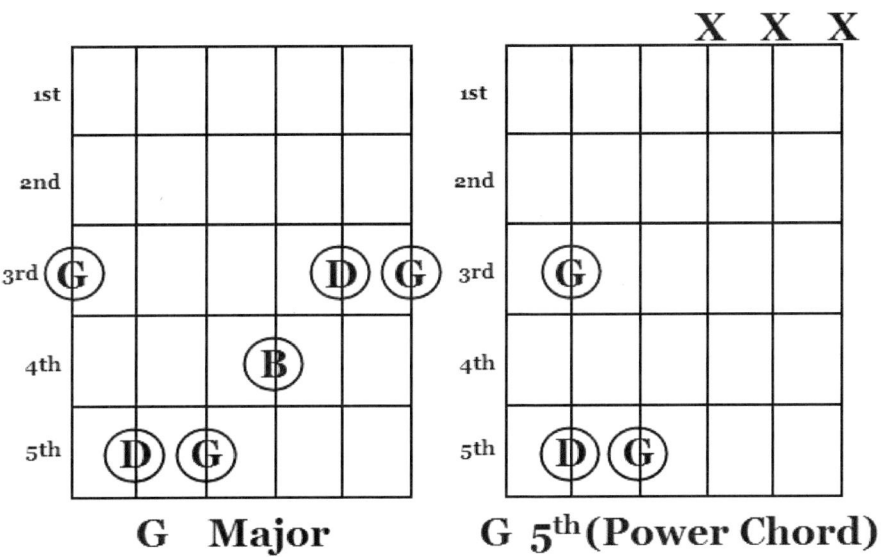

**X = Mute to Deaden,
or Try Not to Play**

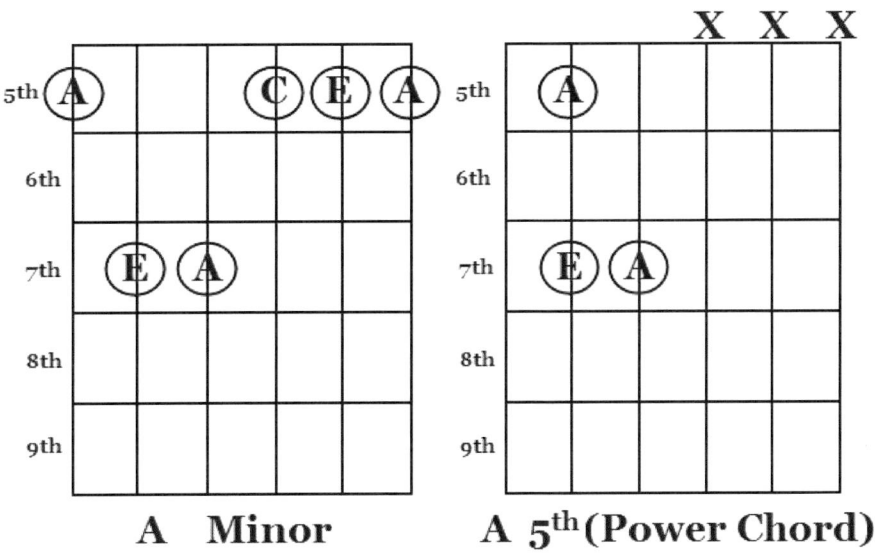

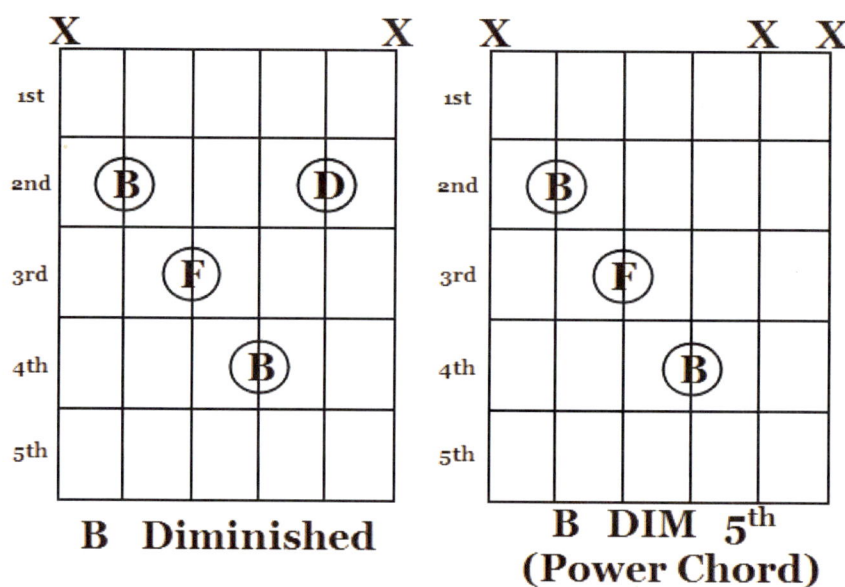

A lot of power chords are played in a chugging method. Listen to any metal song from the 80s, and you'll know it's true, ha-ha. The power chords needed in the C Major scale would be the the following: C, D, E, F, G, and A, while the B would have to be a root and a ♭5th, as shown in the diagrams above and below. (Though most will use a B natural 5th at times when using power chords for proper voicing the B♭ 5th is more tonal.)

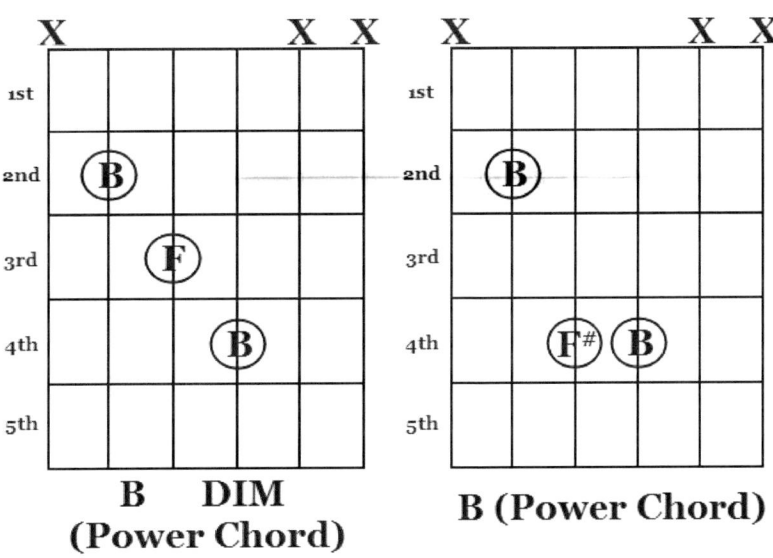

X = Mute to Deaden, or Try Not to Play

B DIM (Power Chord)   **B (Power Chord)**

Though these are in the key of C, depending on which power chords you use, you can play other scales as well. This is done famously in a lot of rock-n-roll and a lot of metal players by playing power chords and using the G Mixolydian mode as their favorite scale to play over them.

Let's say you had a progression of G Major, D Major, and C Major, which is a very standard rock-n-roll progression. Because of the D Major, you couldn't play the C Major scale over that progression. But if we took away the 3^{rd}s and just played the power chords of G, D, and C, you could then play the C Major scale (using the G Mixolydian). You should recall from the previous chapter that the G Mixolydian is a mode in the C Major scale. If not, then review the previous chapter again because all the modes covered in the previous weeks are needed to enhance tonalities. Refer to the diagram below to see how G Mixolydian is played on the fretboard:

42 | A Lesson A Week: *The Theory of Guitar Made Easy*

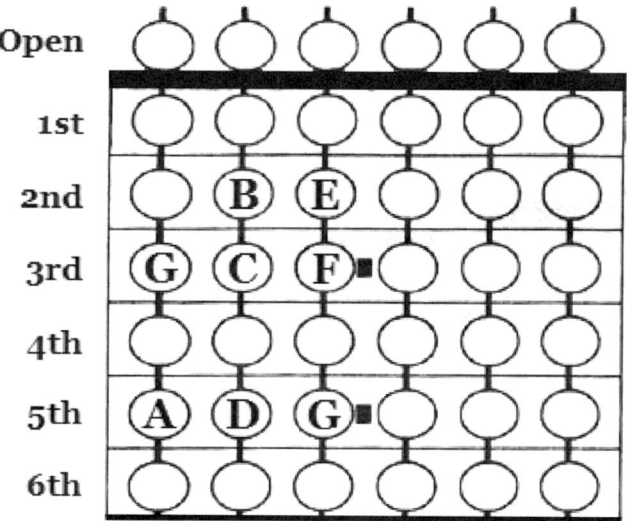

G Mixolydian

One should note that when playing the power chords of G, D, and C, you could also play the G Major scale over it as long as you didn't play the F power chord. If you do a little homework, you'll also notice that most any other progression in C Major played as power chords would fit in the G Major scale. The G, the A, the B, the C, the D, and the E; anything but the F.

That is the beauty of power chords; they can be played throughout various mode, both Major and Minor. When we get into chromatic scales, using power chords will be a very handy tool. While it's hard to play chromatics over a normal chord pattern, they can become useful flavoring to a power chord pattern, which is used a lot in heavy metal. Refer to the diagram below to understand the G Major scale pattern before moving on:

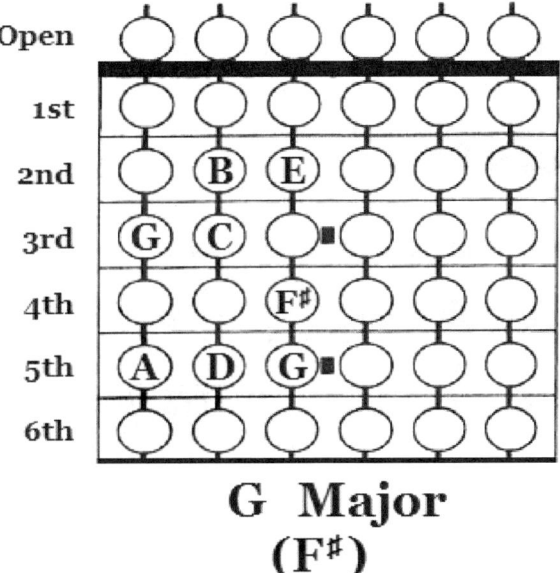

G Major
(F♯)

Let's look at another Major scale, F Major, which would fit in our D, G, C, pattern. The F Major, where again, as long as you didn't use the B power chord in the progression, proves that the F Major scale works fine with the power chords G, A, C, D, and E. Look at the diagram below:

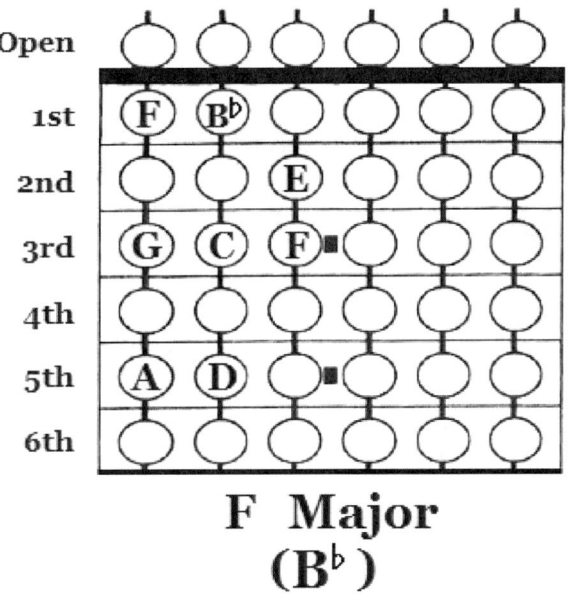

F Major
(B♭)

You might notice that by leaving out a B and an F power chord, you can play the C Major scale, the G Major scale, and the F Major scale, all over power chords of C, D, E, G, and A. The problem is that you wouldn't switch between the F and the G Major scales; but you might switch the tonalities between the C Major and the F Major, and the C Major and G Major, giving you two different scalular patterns to play between (adding fourteen modes all together). This is how powerful power chords and suspended chords (which have either a 2nd or a 4th replacing the 3rd) can be in your playing. Look at the diagrams below to see how you can switch between tonalities:

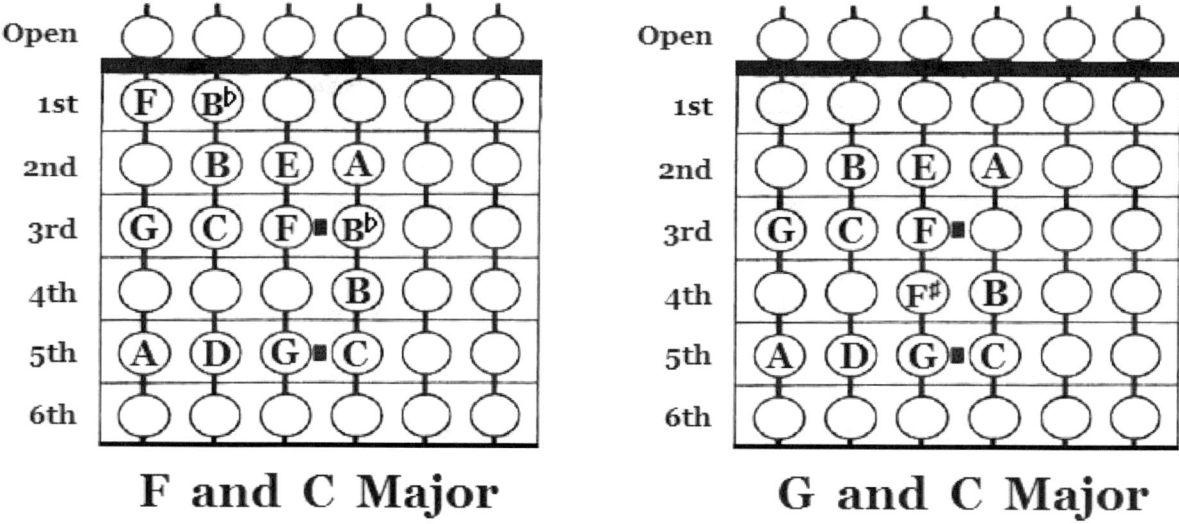

F and C Major   G and C Major

This also adds a chromatic flavor you can play with those scales. In the case of the F and C Major scales, the extra chromatic notes that can be played are B♭, B, and C. With the case of the G and C Major scales, the extra chromatic notes are F, F♯, and G. Now these notes can be used for flavor to your soloing, or used as an actual segway between the scales (the F and the C, and the G and the C) as a way to smoothly switch between the two scales.

You will notice sometimes, depending on the progression, that when players play a power chord and add a suspended 2nd or even a suspended 4th, it simply means to take away the 3rd and add the 2nd in the pattern, or add the 4th. (You should already know this.) By staying away from the 3rd in chords, it frees you from the problems associated with Major and Minor progressions and gives you a repertoire of scales and modes to enhance your playing freedom that can be mixed and matched. If you look at the diagrams below, you'll see how simple it is to alter a chord, such as A Minor or D Minor, by adding a suspended 2nd and 4th and leaving out the 3rd. Study the diagrams below before moving on:

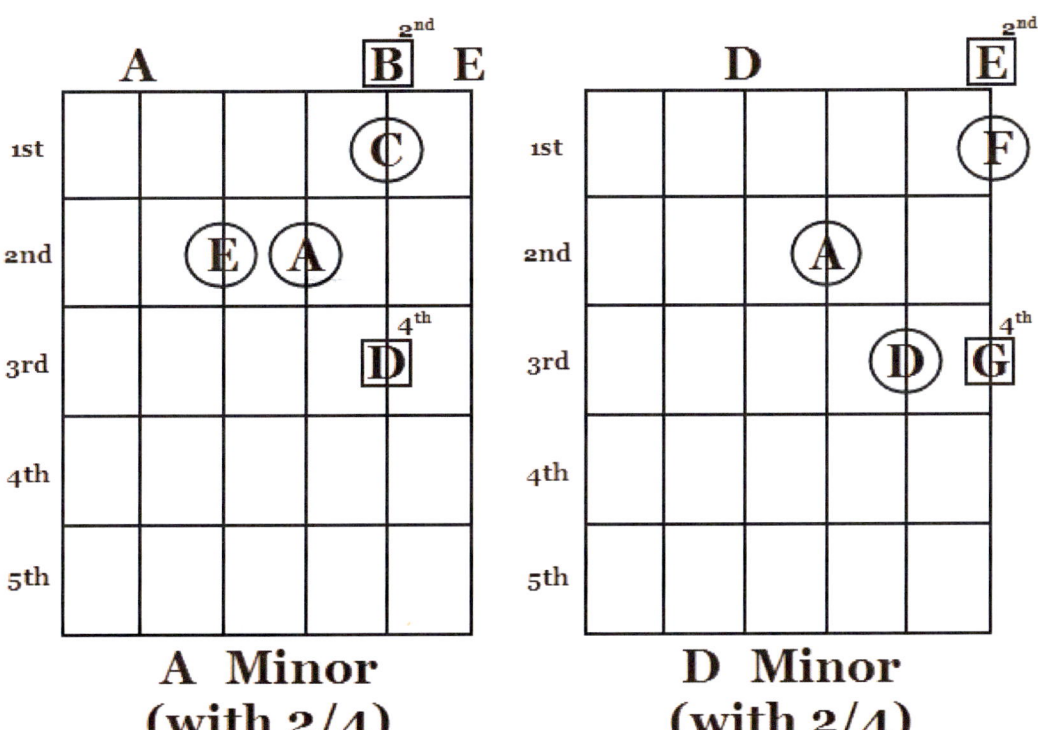

When we get to the Circle of Fifths, we will see what sharps and flats are in all of the Major scales. By analyzing this Circle of Fifths, it will tell us which power chords can be played with which scales. Remember, the ease of playing power chords is simply to remove the 3rd. This will hold true for all chord patterns in every scale.

That's a lot to take in this week, but I know you can handle it. Study all of the diagrams in Week Five, try each power chord out on your guitar, and reread this section until you know and understand the simplicity of power chords.

WEEK SIX: AN INTRODUCTION TO ARPEGGIOS

As an introduction to arpeggios, I'm going to give you seven arpeggios that can be played in the C Major scale. You will only have to transpose arpeggios to make them play in any key. You should remember that transposing is the act of moving into the position needed for the predominant scale.

Arpeggios is just a fancy term, as you have read, for a broken chord. They can be played independently, like a scale, or swept with the pick, making sure to pronounce every single note individually. No matter how fast an arpeggio is swept, it is never strummed in any way, shape, or form, like a chord, even though it is just that, a broken chord.

For these examples we're going to take the basic Major, Minor, and Diminished chords from the C Major scale, starting with the C Major arpeggio, which is C, E, G, C, E, G. Then, the D Minor, which is D, F, A, D, F, A. Followed by the E Minor, which is E, G, B, E, G, B. Bringing us to the F Major, which is F, A, C, F, A, C. Followed by the G Major, which is G, B, D, G, B, D. With the next in line being the A Minor, which is A, C, E, A, C, E. And last, the B Diminished, which is B, D, F, B, D, F. Refer to the diagrams below to review each arpeggio:

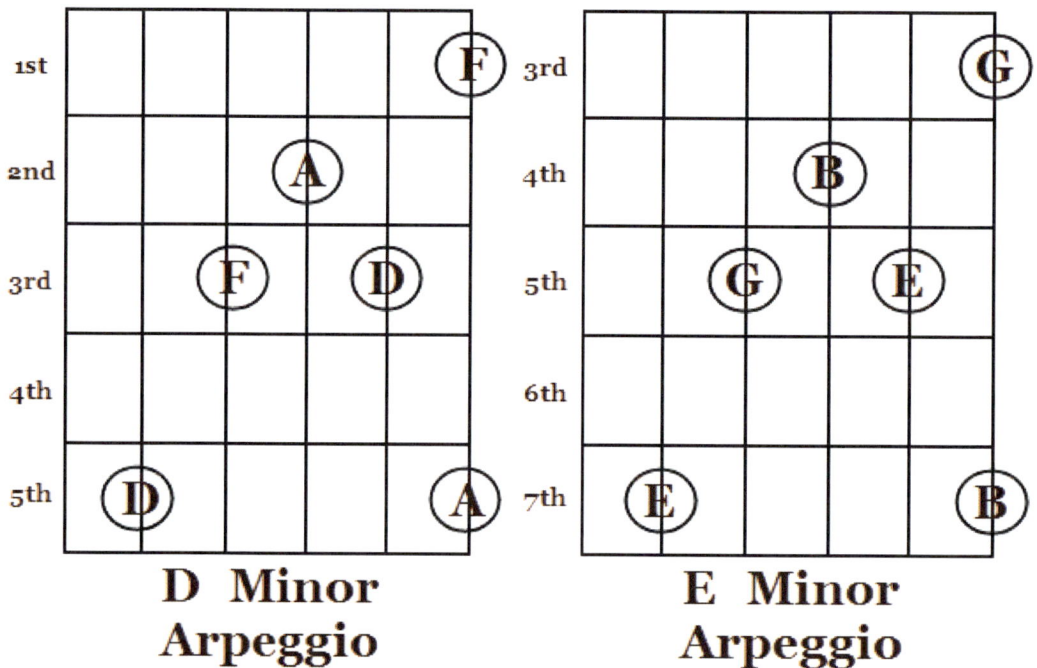

D Minor Arpeggio

E Minor Arpeggio

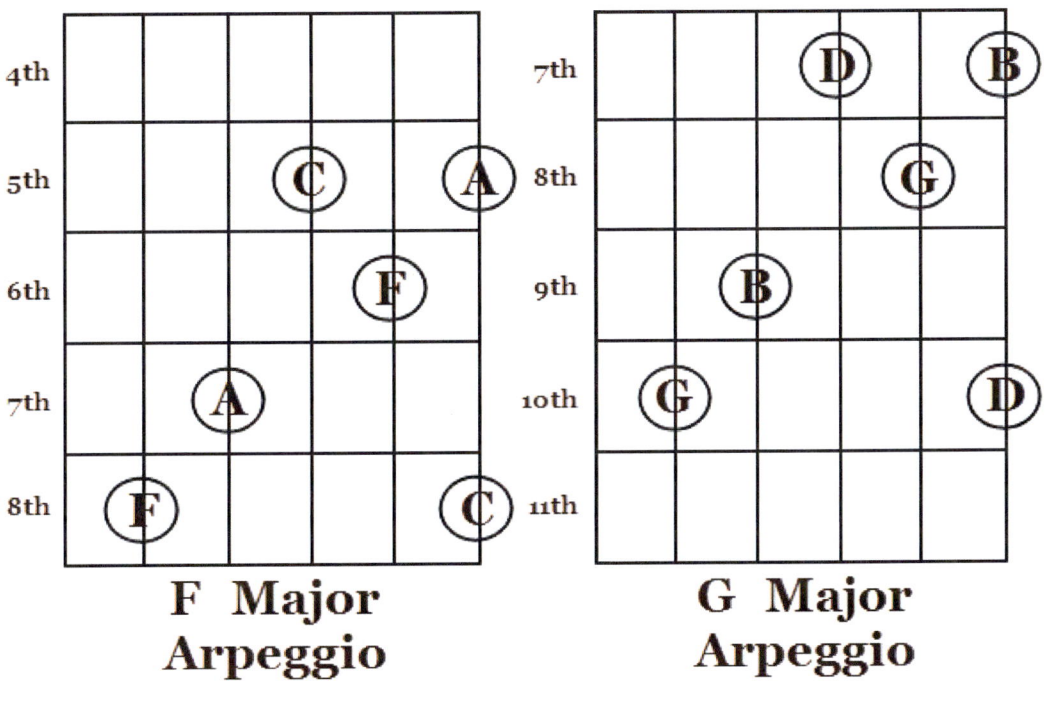
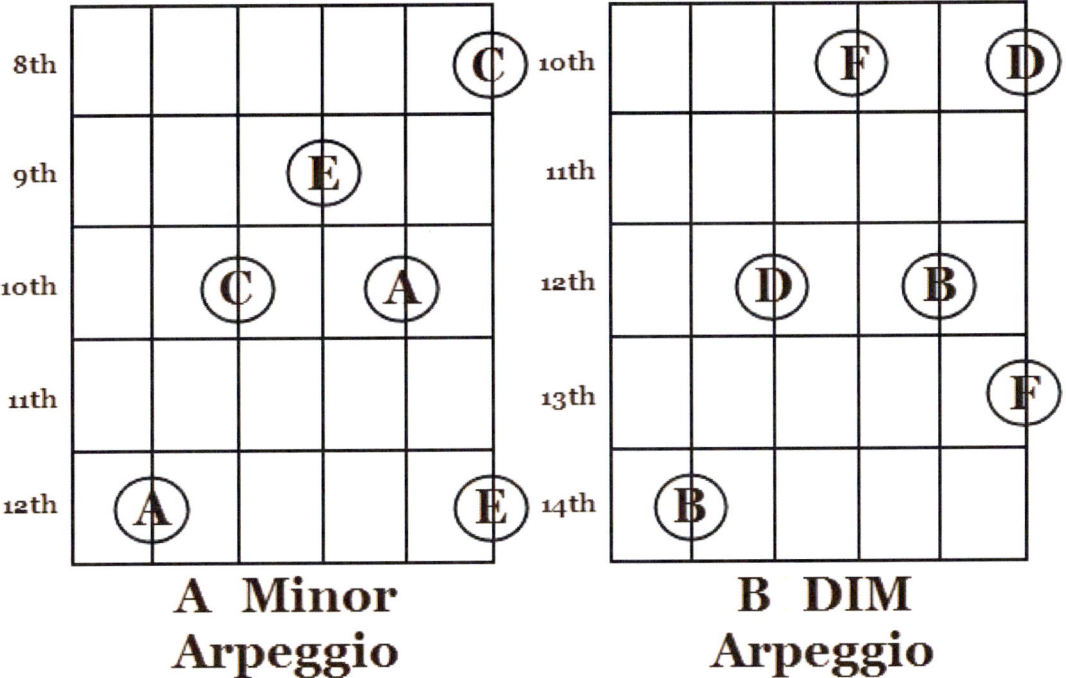

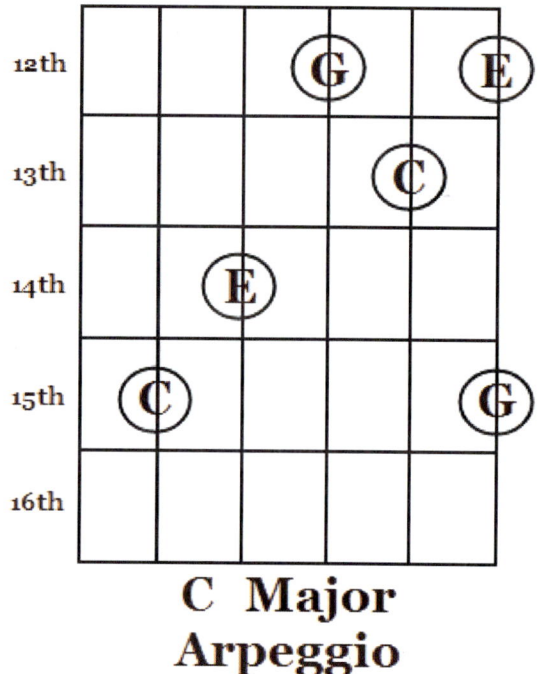

C Major Arpeggio

    You'll practice these arpeggios flowing down the length of the neck. They can be used as a scalular exercise to help you understand the tonality between chords in a Major scale. We can play these patterns elsewhere on the neck, but we're going to give you examples for now based off of the C Major chord; an open position C Major chord. You should know, that bringing the C Major chord down one full step would create the D Major chord. Sharpening the 3rd would make that D Minor a D Major, and by using the same chord pattern you are in fact, sharpening the 3rd.

    Actually we took the form of the open C Major chord and brought it down the neck to create all the chords in the Key of C Major. You could, in fact, do this with other C chords on the neck, repeating the pattern. But I'll leave that to you to experiment with. You don't have to experiment with just a Major chord. Some players use all kinds of chords to break into their arpeggios as we did above. Arpeggio playing differs from intervallic playing by the fact that you would play intervals of a scale pattern instead of chords.

    I'm hoping with this understanding you'll start to realize that there are a lot more positions for playing chords than just the seven open chords and the few various bar chords brought down the length of the neck. Refer to the diagrams below to view some other arpeggios positionings:

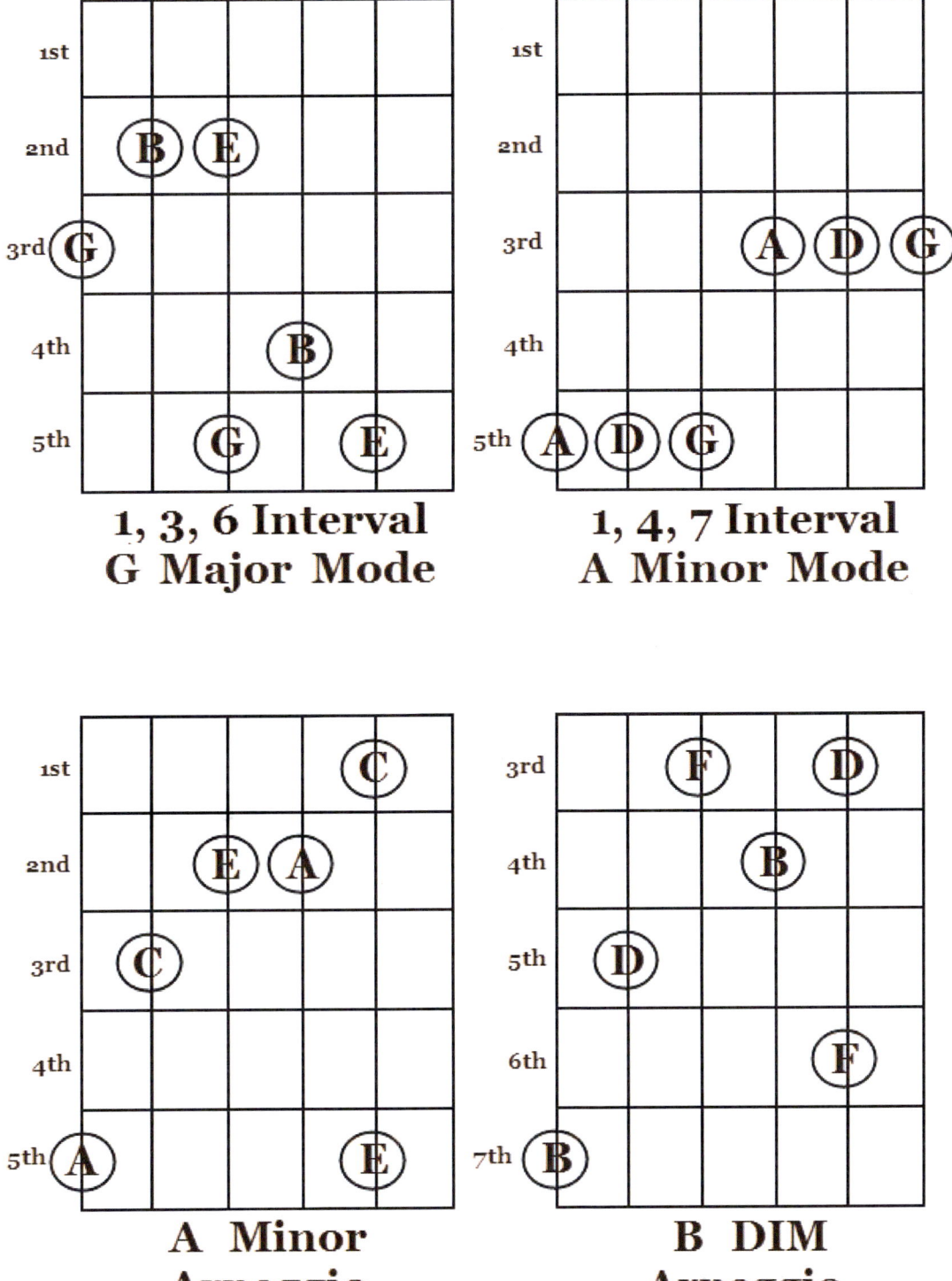

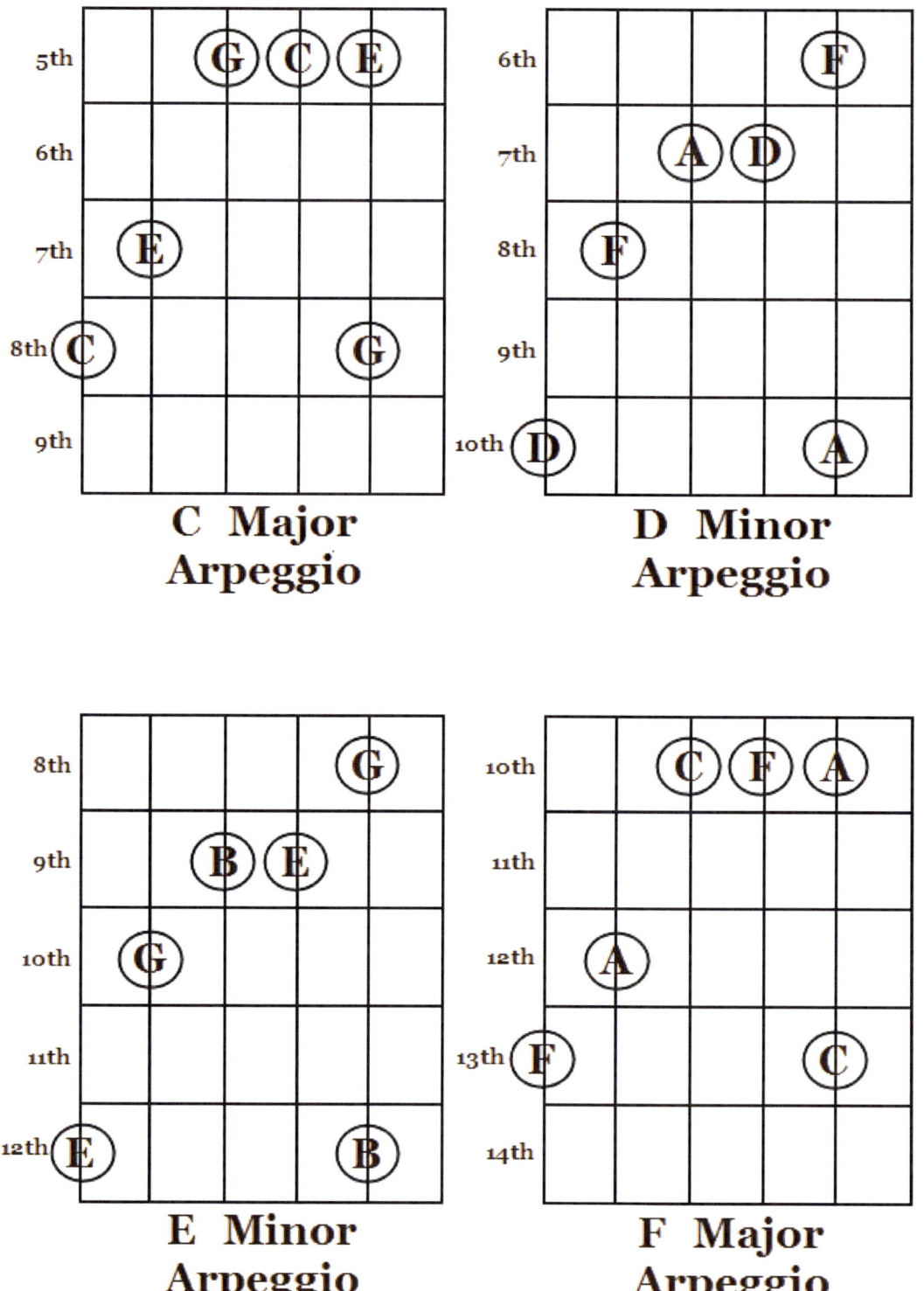

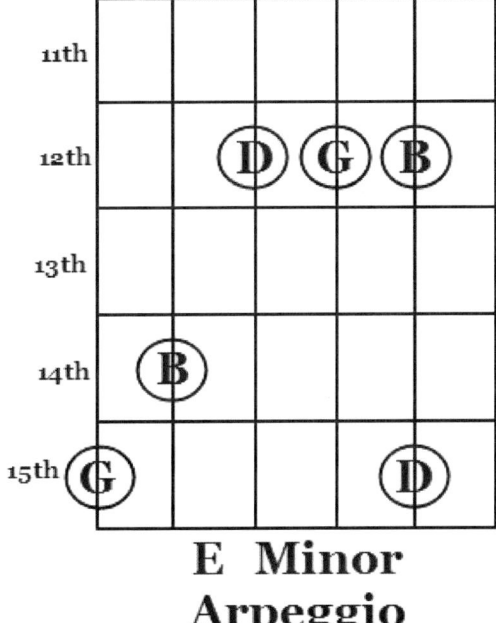

E Minor Arpeggio

Take your time reviewing and practicing these arpeggios every day this week. In fact, you should also be practicing what you have learned from previous weeks. Only by repeatedly practicing ALL the materials we've covered thus far will make what you've learned become permanent. See you in a week.

WEEK SEVEN: THE CIRCLE OF FIFTHS

Welcome to a new week of mastering guitar theory. This week, we will cover the Circle of Fifths, which is a tool used to examine the Major scales to learn which Sharps and Flats are used in each scale. The Circle of Fifths is laid out in such a way that it goes from the C Major at the top, having no Sharps or Flats, all the way down to the bottom, which is labeled. G♭/F♯, which contains the most Sharps and Flats. It should be noted that when two notes, such as G♭/F♯, sound exactly the same, they can be referred to by either name. A note with two names is called an *enharmonic*. This particular enharmonic on the Circle of Fifths is the only one that uses six Flats for the G♭, as well as using six Sharps for the F♯. Look at the diagram below to review the C Major position and the G♭/F♯ position:

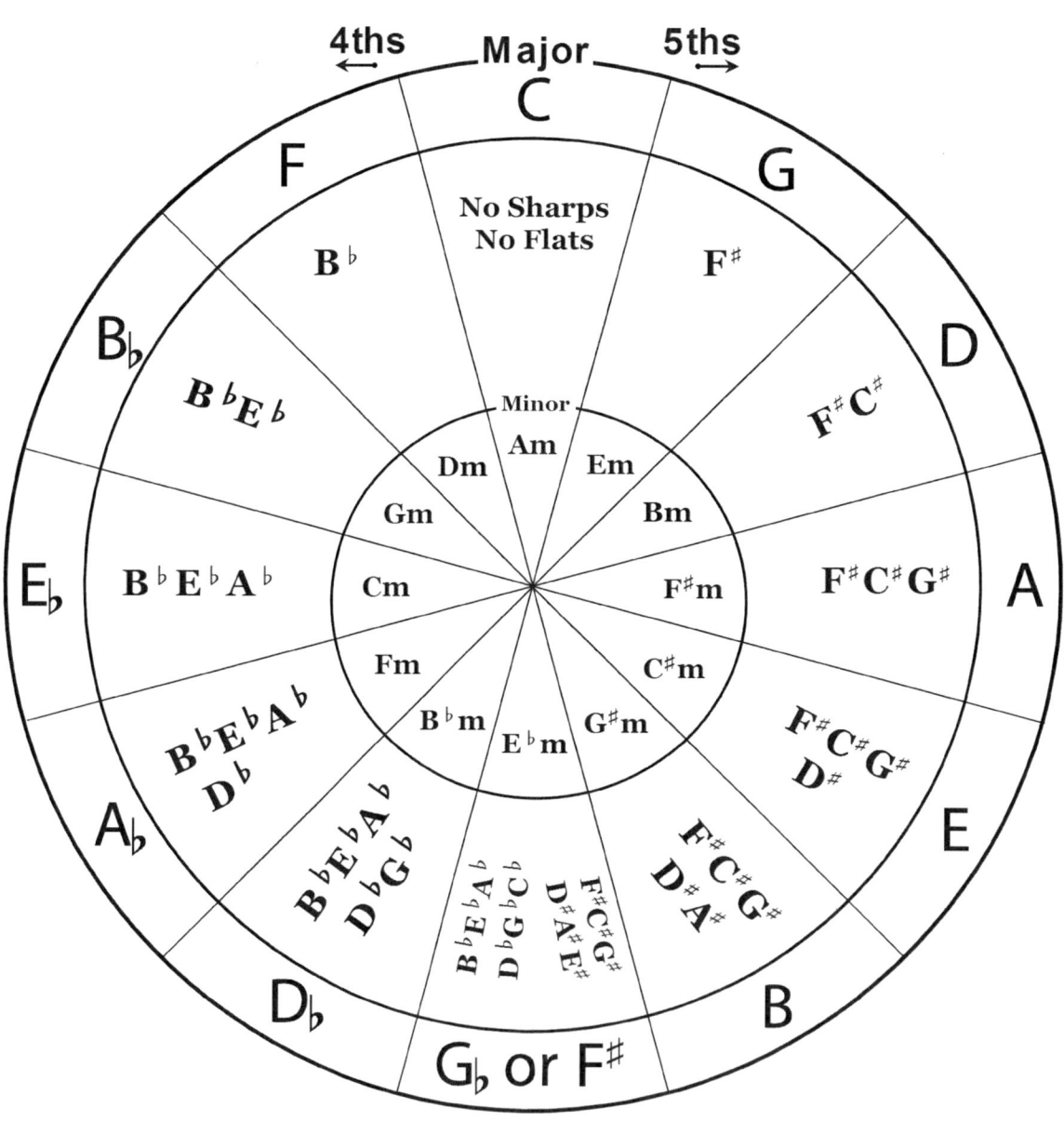

Let's continue looking at the Circle of Fifths diagram above. Beginning at the progression to the top right side, you will see that it goes from one Sharp-G Major, two Sharps-D Major, three Sharps-A Major, four Sharps-E Major, five Sharps-B Major, ending with the dual bottom of the circle with six Sharps for the F♯ Major.

You will notice that the 5th of the first Major scale, the C Major, is the G Major scale with one Sharp. The next is the 5th of G Major, which is the D Major scale with two Sharps. Then, the 5th of D Major, which is the A Major scale with three Sharps. Then, the 5th of that the E Major scale with four Sharps. Then, the 5th of E Major, which is the B Major scale with five Sharps. Then, the 5th of the B Major, which the last of the Sharps, the F♯ with six Sharps.

We then have to substitute the F♯ with the G♭ to continue around the Circle of Fifths, because the 5th of F♯ wouldn't fit exactly right into our method of remembering. (Actually, it would, but it is easier to substitute it with G♭.)

Changing from F♯ to the G♭, which has six Flats, we would now move to the next 5th, which is D♭ (in the same clockwise direction working back up to C Major on the left side) which has five Flats. Then, to the next 5th, which is the A♭ with four Flats. Then, to the next 5th, which is the the E♭ with three Flats. Then, to the next 5th, which is B♭ with two Flats. Then, to the next 5th, which is F Natural with one Flat. We go one more 5th, which takes us back to the starting top C Natural, with no Sharps or Flats (no ♯ or ♭).

I hope understand that by saying, "to the 5th" or "to the next 5th", you are actually moving to the 5th note in the series of the preceding Major scale. The first five notes to the 5th of the C Major is C, D, E, F, G. You are going to the 5th note to get the 5th, which leads us to G Major. I hope you see the pattern. Just in case it is still a little confusing, I'll give you one more, just to be sure you see the pattern. Then, it is up to you to complete the rest. The fifth note of G Major is G, A, B, C, D, which leads us to D Major. The first five notes to the next 5th of the D Major is, D, E, F♯, G, A, which leads us to A as the 5th. Now I would like for you to finish this little exercise. However, if needed, you can use the diagram below until you fully understand this concept:

SCALE:

C Major No ♯s, No ♭s	C	D	E	F	G	A	B	C
G Major 1 ♯	G	A	B	C	D	E	F♯	G
D Major 2 ♯s	D	E	F♯	G	A	B	C♯	D
A Major 3 ♯s	A	B	C♯	D	E	F♯	G♯	A
E Major 4 ♯s	E	F♯	G♯	A	B	C♯	D♯	E
B Major 5 ♯s	B	C♯	D♯	E	F♯	G♯	A♯	B
F♯ Major 6 ♯s	F♯	G♯	A♯	B	C♯	D♯	E♯	F♯
G♭ Major 6 ♭s	G♭	A♭	B♭	C♭	D♭	E♭	F	G♭
D♭ Major 5 ♭s	D♭	E♭	F	G♭	A♭	B♭	C	D♭
A♭ Major 4 ♭s	A♭	B♭	C	D♭	E♭	F	G	A♭
E♭ Major 3 ♭s	E♭	F	G	A♭	B♭	C	D	E♭
B♭ Major 2 ♭s	B♭	C	D	E♭	F	G	A	B♭
F Major 1 ♭	F	G	A	B♭	C	D	E	F

You might be wondering why certain note names are missing, such as C♯. There is no C♯ because it is called D♭, no A♯ because it is B♭, etc. Yes, they could be consider enharmonics, but in writing music, we stick to what is displayed on the diagram above.

Also note that if you look at the example of the Circle of Fifths and follow the circle counter-clockwise instead of clockwise from the C Major on top, (or toward the left) it is no longer the Circle of Fifths. It is now called the Circle of Fourths. For example, following counter-clockwise, you'll see that the 4th of C Major is F natural. The 4th of F is B♭, and the 4th of B♭ is E♭, etc,. All the way around the circle.

I had great fun writing this weekly lesson, and I hope you are having fun learning, and that you did indeed, learn something from it :-) Keep studying and I will see you in a week where we will review Chapter Two.

WEEK EIGHT: REVIEW

In this review, think back on all you've learned over the past three weeks. Here is a breakdown on the knowledge you should pertain from Chapter Two:

- How do you suspend a chord?
- What is a power chord?
- What is the G power chord?
- What is an arpeggio?
- Which three notes make up the C Major arpeggio?
- What is the Circle of Fifths?
- How far away from a natural note is the sharp of that note?
- Which note would you add to make a C Suspended 2nd and which note would you remove?
- Name all the power chords in the C Major scale?
- Transpose the chords in the C Major scale to D Major.
- Name all the power chords in the F Major scale?
- Which three notes can be used to flavor any C Major progression when using the C and G Major scales, to segway into the change of scales?
- What makes up the D Minor arpeggio and note positions? (Ex: 1st, 2nd, 3rd, 4th, etc..)
- What is meant by a natural 5th?
- What other note is A♯ a substitute for?
- What natural note could E♯ be represented by?

Study hard this week and make sure you know all the materials from from the first two chapters before moving on to Chapter Three.

CHAPTER THREE: EXOTIC SCALES & MODES

Chapter Three will advance you deeper into the world of guitar theory. By expanding your thinking beyond the basics, you're starting to have more creative freedom to explore your musical visions. Hopefully, this has been a help to you so far. Let's review what each week of Chapter Three will cover and review terms and questions that are important to these weeks, such as, "What is the bridge of a song?" and "chord shuffling". Let's review:

Week Nine: Mixing Scales and Modes
Week Nine focuses on the breakdown of where and why you would play certain modes throughout a progression.

Week Ten: Harmonic Minor, Melodic Minor, Diminished scales
Week Ten is an introduction to the more flamboyant scales and their use.

Week Eleven: Chromatic Scales
Week Eleven will explain how the use of chromatic scales can come into play.

Week Twelve: Review
During this final week of Chapter Three, you will review what you've learned from the previous weeks of this chapter.

Before We Get Started
Now, let's review some basic terms that can be applied to our Chapter Three studies.

What is chord shuffling?
Chord shuffling simply refers to shuffling or chugging a chord progression instead of repeating the same progression, that would change the structure of the key the scales or chords are in. It might not be done during the whole progression but part of it, like the bridge.

What is a bridge?
A bridge in a song is a change from the progressions of the chords, (sometimes in a different key, though the key does not have to change), that creates a total break musically from everything else in the song, such as between the verse and chorus. Often, it might lead from the verse to the chorus of a song, thus creating a "bridge" from the verse to chorus.

What is ascending?
When you play a group of chords, notes, or scales in an upward progression, like A to B or C to D, but never backwards like G to F, this is considered, "ascending." A to F to G would still be ascending, though we skip notes. It doesn't matter if it is in sequential order (A, B, C, D) just as long as you are ascending upwards (B, D, E, G).

What is descending?
Descending is the exact reverse of ascending, where you would go backward, such as in D to C to A.

What is Chromatic?
We've covered this term before, but it needs repeating. Chromatic refers to ALL twelve notes of the scale. There are two ways to look at chromatic. First, you could look at it as a half step of every note, in other words, to play A, A♯, B, C, C♯, D, D♯, E, F, F♯, G, G♯, back to A. Second, you can look at chromatic as a partial half step added in some patterns, as in a chromatic run, like we explained when mixing two unique scales with crossover notes.

What is blending of tones?
A blending of tones is any mixture of chords or notes that blend well together because of being in a particular key.

What is tonic in music?
The tonic is the main note in any key. It's sometimes also called the key note. The tonic can also refer to the chord built on the first scale degree. In C Major, C is the

tonic, and the C Major chord is the tonic chord.

Reread these terms before proceeding to Week Nine. When you are ready, proceed to further your guitar theory knowledge.

WEEK NINE: MIXING SCALES & MODES

This week, we will look at mixing scales with modes. Modes can be played at times, like in jazz, with particular chords, to enhance the chord tonality behind the run or mode. See the diagram below, based out of C Major, for a reminder of each mode, starting with C Ionian, then D Dorian, to E Phrygian, to F Lydian, to G Mixolydian, to Aeolian, and B Locrian.

R = Root of Major Key the Mode is in

Mode:														
Ionian	R		2		3	4		5		6		7		
Dorian	2		3	4		5		6		7	R			
Phrygian	3	4		5		6		7	R		2			
Lydian	4		5		6		7	R		2		3		
Mixolydian	5		6		7	R		2		3	4			
Aeolian	6		7	R		2		3	4		5			
Locrian	7	R		2		3	4		5		6			

For an exercise, let us examine the Dorian mode, which is the second mode down in the diagram above. Since it is the second mode and we are based out of C Major, we know to first play a D note, which we also know is the root forming a Minor chord. When starting at D, playing the Dorian Mode, you will notice the blending of tones in a different pattern gives it a completely different sound even while playing the same notes. It changes the mood of the scale mode.

Next, let's jump to the fifth mode on our diagram to play a G Major chord, which is G Mixolydian. You will again notice the blend in the tonic mixture of these.

Okay, let us jump back to the E Phrygian, which requires us to first play an E Minor chord. If we move to F Lydian, it is played with an F Major chord. The A Aeolian is played over the A Minor chord. (I am jumping around on purpose to make you think.)

Now we come to a minor problem with Locrian scale. In actuality, you could play the B diminished scale over the B diminished chord, (which we will explain in the next chapter.) But for now, we will stick with the Locrian scale, since it follows the pattern we are using of all natural notes starting with B.

If you pause and remember back to the week where we were playing suspended thirds, (power chords) you will realize that you can now actually play the F Major and C Major scales and modes, OR the G and C Major scales, over each of those same chords with them suspended, or suspending by adding a 2nd or a 4th. However, will need a little watching out when adding the 2nd or 4th to remain in key of the scales and modes we are using.

Let's take a look at the C suspended chord to help make sense of it all. Try playing a F Major over a C Major chord, while playing the F Lydian, with a B♭, instead of B. You will now start to see how the F Lydian can be played instead of the C Major Ionian, thus giving you three modes to play over the C suspended chord. You should now see that every suspended chord would have three modes to be played through, and, depending on the bass parts, you could have a fourth, which is the major of the chord itself, like when we look at the D suspended. This can become very complex because you could start adding the Major and Minor modes to that as well,

In fact, let's do that with the D suspended. While playing D suspended, you could play D Dorian mode, G Dorian Mode, D Major Ionian, G Mixolydian. Pause now and play all four modes against the D Suspended to hear how each mode blends. By understanding and applying this concept, you will have a repertoire of modes to compare, to then choose what your ear likes best.

There is a LOT to take in during this week. So, your focus this week is to read and reread this lesson as you practice walking through each mode on your fretboard, using the diagram in this lesson as your guide. It is imperative you put in the work this week to remember the patterns and understand the relationship before moving on to Week Ten.

Now that you have a glimpse of what you can really do with scales, modes, chords, suspended chords added against a background of tones, you can begin to open up and expand your playing with all of this knowledge. So, study hard and I will see you in a week.

WEEK TEN: HARMONIC MINOR, MELODIC MINOR & DIMINISHED SCALES

Week Ten is an introduction to the more flamboyant scales and their use. I am only going to touch on these scales to familiarize you with them, because in reality, you could write an entire book on each of these scales and how they can be used, which may be the case for a future book. Let's review each scale:

Harmonic Minor Scales

The Harmonic Minor scale comes into play by using the A Aeolian. By sticking with the C Major scale yet again, we have to alter the the 7th of the A Minor Aeolian mode, which is the G natural note, by sharpening it a half-step. So, instead of A, B, C, D, E, F, G, A, which is the natural Aeolian of the C Major scale, you would now play the Harmonic Minor scale of, A, B, C, D, E, F, G♯, A. Refer to the diagram below:

SCALE:

A Aeolian No ♯s, No ♭s	A		B	C		D		E	F		G
A Harmonic Minor 1 ♯	A		B	C		D		E	F			G♯

With this one change, a new chord for the progression will be used to help with the tonic quality; the E Major chord for the Harmonic Minor instead of the E Minor chord for the A Aeolian. Why? Because the added G♯ changes the chord in the scale from an E Minor to an E Major, which gives you the flavor you need for the Harmonic Minor. The chords you will now use are Major C, E, F, G, chords, Minor D and A chords, with a Diminished B chord.

All suspended chords of those chords can be used as well, C, D, E, F, G, A, B. The chromatic notes of G, G♯, A, can also be used in ANY mode of C for flavor. Any mode of the C Major scale can be played by adding the G♯ in place of the G. Refer to the diagram below to review each mode played with G♯:

Modes of C Major with G♯ instead of G

MODE:

C Ionian	C		D		E	F		G♯	A	B
D Dorian	D		E	F		G♯	A		B	C
E Phrygian	E	F		G♯	A		B	C		D
F Lydian	F		G♯	A		B	C		D	E
G Mixolydian	G♯	A		B	C		D		E	F
A Aeolian	A		B	C		D		E	F	G♯
B Locrian	B	C		D		E	F		G♯	A

To review, you can play any mode of the C Major scale as a Harmonic Minor by sharpening the G to G♯ or by adding the G♯ for flavor, playing it with the G for chromatic runs. You can also play all C Major chord patterns by replacing the E Minor with an E Major or with an E Suspended.

Melodic Minor Scales

Now, we'll move onto the Melodic Minor scale. Be afraid, be very afraid. WHY? Because the Melodic Minor is a scale invented to test you. The Melodic Minor scale is played two different ways, depending on which direction you are playing it. Like the Harmonic Minor scale, it too is taken from the Natural Minor A Aeolian (in C Major). Now we must sharpen the 6th and the 7th, but ONLY in the ascending direction, or as you ascend the scale. When in the descending direction, or descending the scale, you go back to playing JUST the A Aeolian.

So, that you fully understand what I just wrote, and to see how this scale will test you, remember that you will play, A, B, C, D, E, F♯, G♯, A in the ascending direction and A, G, F, E, D, C, B, A in the reverse (descending) direction for this Melodic Minor scale. Refer to the diagram below for quick reference:

Melodic Minor

Ascending	A		B	C	D	E	F♯	G♯
Descending	A	G		F	E	D	C	B

How does this affect your playing? It alters chords. For instance, E Major and D Major are substituted in for E Minor and D Minor, BUT ONLY while you are ascending the scame. Those chords are then switched back to E Minor and D Minor while descending.

FYI- you could make it easy and just play E and D suspended and not worry about them in either direction. This kind of chord shuffling can be cool if you watch what you are doing, but would add some interesting tonic flavors if you're spot-on with your mode changes, since you do have to change the F♯ and G♯ in all your modes for the C Major scale EXCEPT in ascending, and back on-the-fly to F and G when playing in descending for all the modes.

To sum it all up, the Melodic Minor scale is created by adding F♯ and G♯ to any C Major mode in ascending only, and then returning to F and G natural when you play any modes while descending. This also means that you will substitute D Major and E Major while ascending, reverting back to D Minor and E Minor chords when descending...or playing it safe and simply playing the D Suspended and the E Suspended in the chord progression. WHEW. Sounds complicated, but it will get easier as you study. Now, onto Diminished scales.

Diminished Scales

A Diminished scale is a very unique scale, and not to be confused with the Locrian Diminished scale from the modes, which is a diminished mode because of the flatted 3rd and flatted 5th diminishing the mode. What we are focusing on is the true Diminished scale.

There are only three true sets of Diminished scales. The reason for this is that the Diminished scale is made up of the following pattern, whole-step, half-step, whole-step, half-step, always alternating and always starting with a whole-step from the Root. So, here is the tricky part...Remember in C Major, we said that you could play the B Locrian or the Diminished Locrian scale. Well, that was actually misleading. You would actually play a half-step from B and start with the C Diminished scale for the C Major scale, if using a B Diminished chord.

This whole section of your studies is made up of scales that make you say, "WHAT?!?!"

I know; crazy, isn't it! But, this is how theory sometimes takes a curve and why a lot of playing can get very complex with tonal flavoring. Now, to add more to this insanity, it is also made up of eight tones, not the standard seven we have seen so far. For if you follow the pattern out, you get eight different tonal notes.So, let's take a look at the three Diminished scales for a better understanding:

The First Diminished Scale, will have the different roots, C, E♭, G♭, or A, but would still be the exact same scales, only with a different starting root, but using the exact same notes, C, D, E♭, F, G♭, A♭, A, B, C. This means you will play that exact same scale starting at those different notes, like you did with modes, to have the first Diminished scale.

The next Diminished scale is the C♯, E, G, or B♭. Again, with all the same notes, but with a different starting root, C♯, D♯, E, F♯, G, A, B♭, C, C♯.

The last Diminished scale roots are D, F, A♭, or B - with the notes D, E, F, G, A♭, B♭, B, C♯, D. Refer to the diagram below to compare all three Diminished scales:

Potential Root → **3 Diminished Scales**

*		*		*		*		
C	D	E♭	F	G♭		A♭	A	B
C♯	D♯	E	F♯	G		A	B♭	C
D	E	F	G	A♭		B♭	B	C♯

Now, let's break it all down by using the whole-step and half-step pattern to see where the notes come from. With only three real scale patterns to learn, just with different starting points and the same Whole, Half, Whole, Half, alternating pattern, you might think the Diminished scale would be an easy one to use. Remember, the starting points will always be the same distance away, so using the pattern in the example, starting with the C, whole-step to D, half-step to E♭, whole-step to F, half-step to G♭, whole-step to A♭, half-step to A, whole-step to B (then a Half-Step to C again). Remember, the roots to that exact first Diminished scale are, C, E♭, G♭, and A. The second Diminished scale will start with C♯ and follow that same pattern of whole and half steps to go, C♯, D♯, E, F♯, G, A, B♭, C (to the C♯ again). The four roots for the second Diminished Scale are, C♯, E, G, and B♭. Remember the same scale just like modes, starting with different starting points for the Roots. The third and last Diminished scale, D, E, F, G, A♭, B♭, B and C♯, with the Roots, D, F A♭, B.

While it is simplistic in using the scale, the trouble comes from the complex nature of using Diminished chords in a progression. Why? Well, as mentioned before, you never want to end a progression on a Diminished chord, because it can make the progression sound unresolved. But this can be resolved, no pun intended. Simply play around with Diminished scales with the root of the songs, using suspended fifths and chords with tones in the Diminished and Major scale you are in. It would be a good way to make them blend.

Alas, this ends the nightmare portion of your introduction of theory. Spend this week working through the variations of Melodic and Harmonic Minor scales, and Diminished scales as applied to each mode based out of C Major.

Reread this week several times to fully get a grasp of the concepts presented in this lesson. Don't let it overwhelm you. I promise, it gets easier and will make ore sense as you practice these concepts.

While I truly believe you can conquer these theory concepts in weekly segments, do not feel pressed to move on to Week Eleven until you've got a solid grasp on these scales. This actually applies to all you've learned so far.

Though we are nearing the end of the book, you MUST understand and remember the concepts you've learned in previous weeks in order to build upon the final weeks and expand your theory expertise. So, if at this point, you feel you need more practice and studying to remember what you've learned so far, there is nothing wrong with going back to earlier weeks to study and apply the concepts, working at your own pace. When you're ready and confident that you've committed to memory everything you've learned in the previous ten weeks, move on to Week Eleven to learn all about Chromatic scales.

WEEK ELEVEN: CHROMATIC SCALES

Ok I lied; we are not done with unusual scales; just the difficult ones, ha-ha. Now we will look at a very, very simplistic scale, the Chromatic scale, and what makes it so simplistic; the fact that the pattern is simply a half-step for each note. That would make our Chromatic scale in our lessons contain C, C♯, D, D♯, E, F, F♯, G, G♯, A, A♯, B, C. It is that simple.

The Chromatic scale is used as a great way to do finger and picking exercises. So, no matter where you start, the actual scale will consist of thirteen consecutive half-step notes. However, you will usually use only a chromatic-run in your solos or as a bridge between changing modes or scales, as I've mentioned before.

Any overuse of chromatics leads to the chance of playing sour tones or just simply playing out of key. Remember, you would not play a Chromatic scale straight across the neck of the guitar; that isn't exactly a Chromatic scale. It still does follow a pattern. For example, if you started on the C note and played the consecutive four notes, the next note in the pattern would not be in the same position of the C (the 8th fret on the E string.) The next would be the E note (the 7th fret on the A string.) Refer to the diagram below to understand this concept:

Chromatic Scale

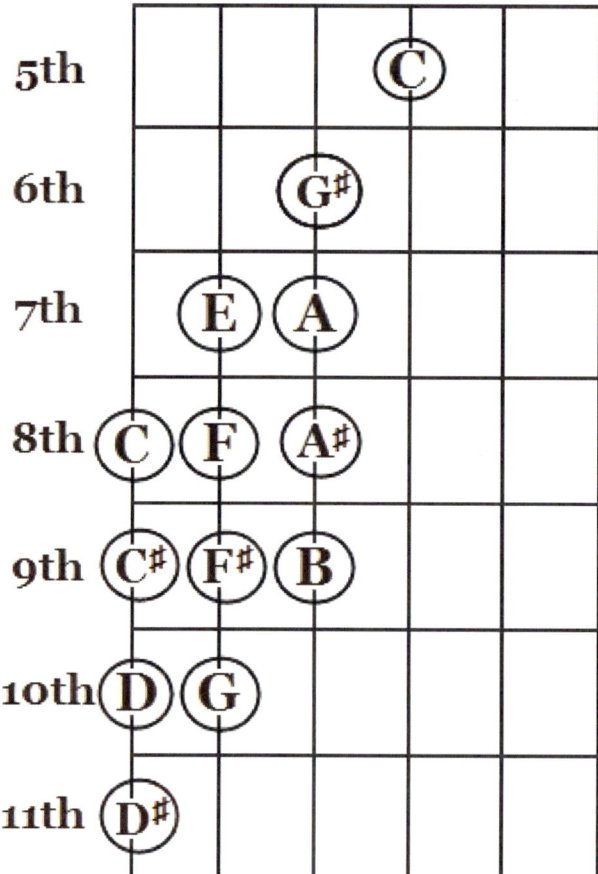

This is a very easy week of study; probably the easiest. This week, take advantage of not only running Chromatic scale patterns in your soloing, but also reviewing the entire book to assure that you have a firm grasp on all the concepts we covered so far.

I do hope you are enjoying this companion series to your music instruction. Study hard and prepare for next week's review of Chapter Three, and know that if you are studying, you are doing great! We only have one more chapter to go. I do hope this has helped you to understand better ways to flavor your playing. See you next week in review.

WEEK TWELVE: REVIEW

You MUST be able to answer the following questions before moving on to Chapter Four. In fact, I HIGHLY suggest you revisit the Review sections for Chapters One and Two to assure you've retained what you've learned in previous weeks as well. If you feel you've worked hard and absorbed all of this theory knowledge like a sponge, then proceed:

- What note would you start with for the Dorian mode in the key of C?
- What is a C suspended chord, also known as a C 5th chord?
- What is the benefit of playing suspended chords?
- What is the difference between an A Aeolian and an A Harmonic Minor scale? What is the difference between the two scales?
  What is the one note that is changed in the C Major scale and all of its modes to make all of its scales and modes Harmonic Minor?
- Is there a difference in the Melodic Minor ascending and descending, and if so what is it?
- How many true Diminished scales are there that are not the same exact scale starting with a different root?
- What do you do to create a Chromatic scale?
- How many notes are in a true Chromatic scale?

Don't fret if you missed a few. This isn't a test. Take your time and dive back into previous weeks until you have a firm grasp on all you've learned so far. Once you're ready, proceed to our final chapter.

CHAPTER FOUR: BLUES VERSUS PENTATONICS

This final chapter will advance you into the world of guitar theory by dealing with an area I feel hard pressed to avoid, because it is too controversial as a whole; Blues versus Pentatonics. Since my goal is to enhance your playing by expanding your thinking beyond, I can't leave out the most important section of all. So, here is your breakdown of the final weeks of study:

Week Thirteen: Pentatonic and Blues Chords and Progressions
Week Thirteen is an introduction to which chords to use for progressions in Pentatonic and Blues playing.

Week Fourteen: Basic Pentatonic Major and Minor scales
Week Fourteen is an introduction to the more flamboyant scales and their use.

Week Fifteen: Mixing it up with the Blues
In Week Fifteen, I'll explain how to mix up Blues scales with Pentatonic scales for an innovative new look into both.

Week Sixteen: Review
During the final week of Chapter Four, you will review what you've learned from the previous weeks of this chapter.

Before We Get Started
Here is your quick preface to questions and terms that might arise during the reading of this chapter:

What are the Blues?
The Blues are something that is definable in a different way by each individual. But, in theory, there are six note scales that give the Blues their flavor, and as you'll soon discover, should not to be confused with the Pentatonics.

What does Pentatonic mean?
Literally, Pentatonic means five tones or five notes. Penta, meaning five. As applied to a scale, a Pentatonic is a five-note Major scale that also use five notes in the Minor version, and are often confused with the Blues scale.

What is the difference between a Major Pentatonic and a Minor Pentatonic?
The positioning of the root and other positions of the same notes will change accordingly to add a Major or Minor flavor to the five note scale.

Is the Blues scale Major or Minor?
The Blues scale is a Minor scale that can still be transposed by transposing the root.

What is the Chromatic run in the Blues scale?
The Blues scale has a Chromatic run between the 4th, flatted 5th, and 5th in the Minor version of its scale. (The Blues should always start with the root in its Minor form.)

Is there a difference in the chord progressions between the Pentatonic scales and the Blues?
Yes. We'll be pointing these out in the chapters ahead, even showing when Diminished chords will come into play.

Once you've reviewed the answers to these questions and understand terms such as, "Pentatonic," you may proceed to Week Thirteen.

WEEK THIRTEEN: BLUES CHORDS & PROGRESSIONS

There is a BIG difference between the actual Blues and Pentatonic scales. First, Pentatonics are just that; "penta" meaning five notes from the Major scale, also using five notes to the Minor pentatonics. Blues scales consist of six notes.

> *"You mean the Blues isn't just Pentatonics? But that is what my friend said when he plays the blues."*

I'm sorry to say, most are mistaken when it comes to scales, modes, and the actual theory behind guitar, especially when it comes to the Blues and Pentatonics. I've even seen incorrect published material from teachers that never bothered to look into what they believe they understand.

This doesn't make them bad at playing. Let's face it; a lot of blues guitar is based solely on feeling and there really is no real theory behind true feeling, just the basics. But if you were highly educated at English Lit, it would make it flow so much easier to write an essay versus someone who just understood the basics of English.

In the end, what you learn will help you express your feelings much better, with more voicings, and more enhancement in your tonalities. Why mention this now? Because unlike anything else we have covered, the Blues are really all about feelings, emotions, and moods.

Still, you might ask, "What about Pentatonics? What makes them different than the Blues?" First off, this question is simply an excuse for some players to explain the, "chops versus feeling" argument. Pentatonics are a nice introduction into the Blues, but in a more formatted way. Still, just because you format your playing does not mean you're playing *without* feeling. It would be more like preparing for a speech. You would want to know what ideas and themes you are trying to inspire with your words. But the true inspiration comes from the delivery of your speech. It is the same with music. If you did not know what ideas or themes or tonic tones beforehand, or know what you were trying to do musically, it could sound pretty uninspiring.

Before moving on, review the diagram below to see the difference between the Pentatonics and a Blues scale.

Key of C Major	A		C		D	E♭	E		G	
Pentatonic Major	6th		R		2nd		3rd		5th	
Pentatonic Minor	R		♭3rd		4th		5th		♭7th	
Blues	R		♭3rd		4th	♭5th	5th		♭7th	

Pentatonic Chords

Now let's take a look at chords with pentatonics, both Major and Minor. Starting with the Major Pentatonic chords, let's look at the scale to find our chords, which consists of the Root, 2nd, 3rd, 5th, and 6th. Keeping in the scale of C Major, you would play C Major or 5th, D Minor or 5th, E Minor or 5th, G Major or 5th, and A Minor or 5th. Remember, 5th refers to suspending the 3rd. These would be the best chords to play to polarize around a C Major Pentatonic. Suspending the 3rd, as we've seen before, frees us up to use a lot of variations. For example, the G Major Pentatonic would fit in as usual. (Remember, we aren't using the F note, which would be sharp in the G Major scale and natural in the C, if we leave out the D Minor or play the D 5th.)

Just for a little review to recall the difference between a chord and a 5th chord, AND to review the five Pentatonic chords, refer to the diagrams below:

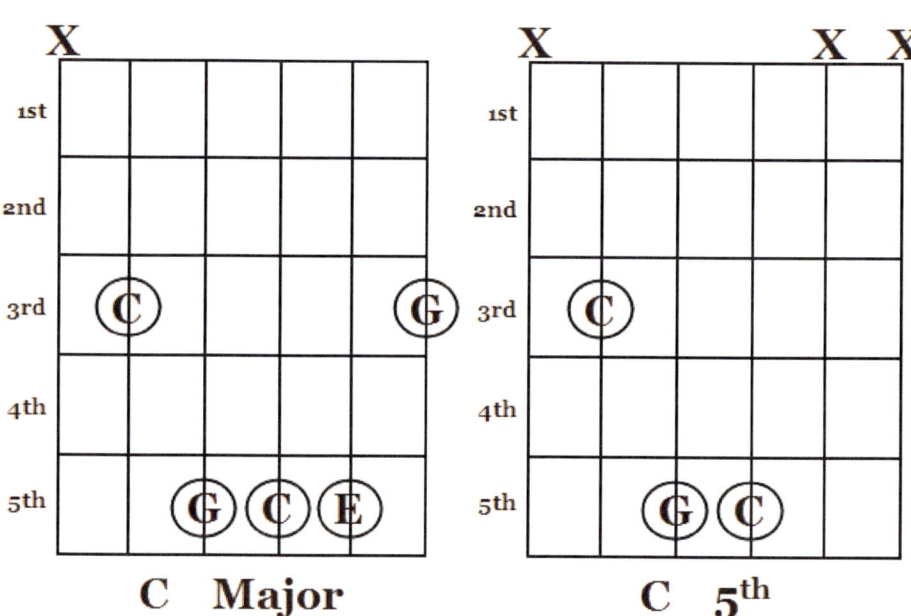

X = Mute dead to Not Play, or Try Not to Play

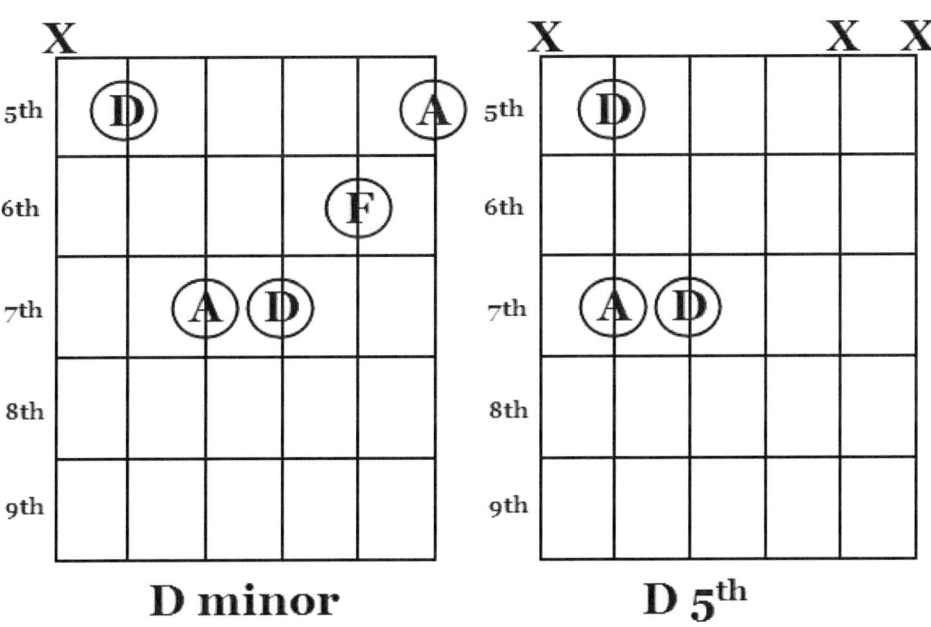

X = Mute to Deaden, or Try Not to Play

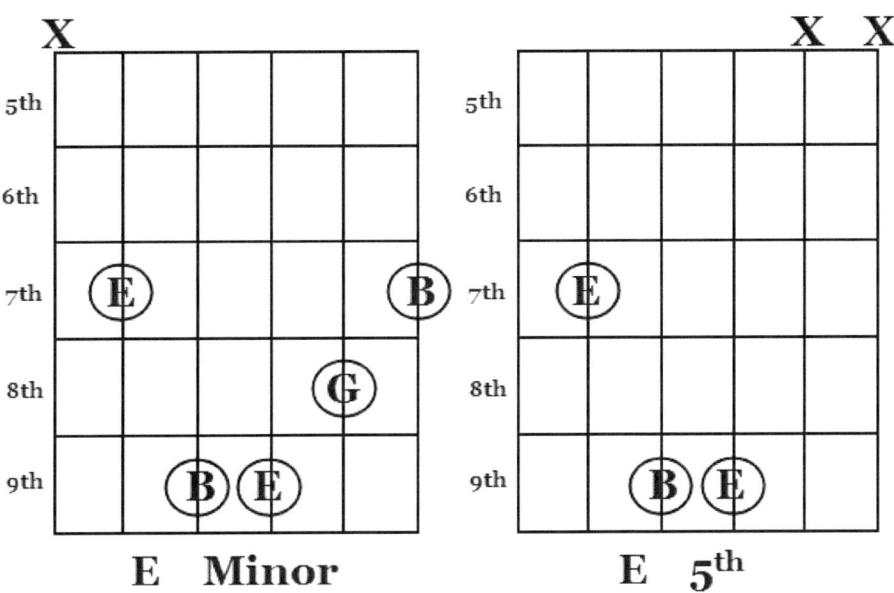

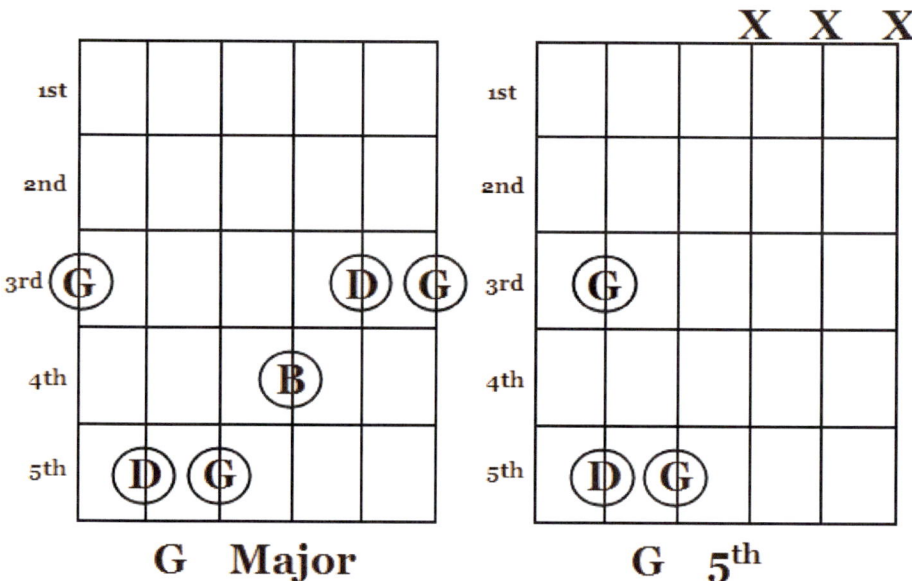

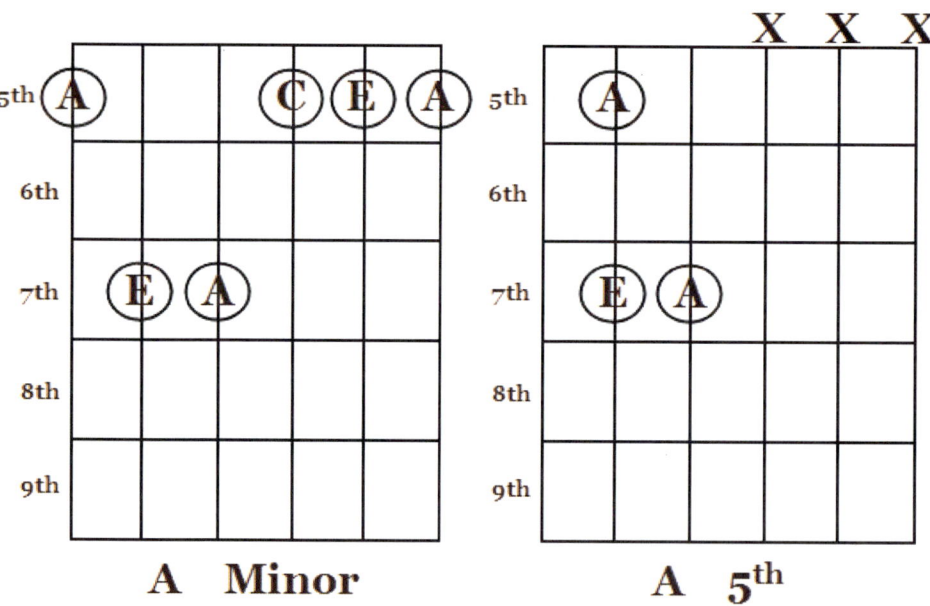

For the Minor Pentatonics, we would have the Root A, ♭3rd C, 4th D, E for the 5th, and lastly the ♭7th of G, all taken from the A Major scale, with the 3rd and 7th flatted to fit into the Minor of the pentatonic scale. So, the chords would again be, A Minor, C Major, D Minor, E Minor and G Major.

"Wait, these are the same chords, so, wouldn't it have been easier to use the A Minor scale for the Pentatonics, taking the 1st, 3rd, 4th, 5th, and 7th from the A Minor mode of the C Major?"

First, let me applaud you. I am so glad you are soaking up all this knowledge and were able to ask me such a great question.

My reply is, "Yes, it would be easier." But, I wanted to show you it whole in both its forms and IF they are the same notes starting in A for the Minor Pentatonic as it is starting in C for the Major Pentatonic.

"Well, why not just simplify it and say, that the Pentatonic Major starts with the Root, in this case, C, and the Pentatonic Minor starts with the 6th, in this case, A."

Precisely! Now you're thinking! That is exactly what you will do. But, again, I wanted to explain it out to you. Theory-wise, there is so much more you can do in flavors and chords- in fact, we could write another entire book on it, and you will start to see the beauty of this mathematical/musical language as you grow in your knowledge.

Before moving on to Blues chords, review the diagrams below to understand the relationship between the Major and Minor Pentatonic progressions:

Blues Chords
Let's take a look at the six Blues chords. But first, a quick reminder. Although we have been based out of C throughout this entire book, do not forget that you can transpose these keys, scales, notes, and chords, so you are far from limited to what is presented in these lessons. But, by learning these patterns, it will help you find keys and extra voicings to add to your playing.

The six Blues notes in the Blues scales are as follows, in the Key of C Major (though the Blues scale is actually a Minor scale.) You would start with Root A, then the ♭3rd, 4th, ♭5th, 5th, and ♭7th or A, C, D, D♯, E, and G.

You will notice the actual Blues scale has a chromatic run, consisting of D, D♯, E, which is something that true Pentatonics don't have. This chromatic run makes it unique from the actual Major Scale, or Minor Mode. Because of this extra chromatic note, a lot of voicings are possible.

Now, let's cover each note as it forms a chord, breaking down which chords can be applied in the Blues scale.

Starting with A Minor or A 5th, or how about A Diminished- A, the root of the Minor scale, C the ♭3rd, and D♯ the ♭5th. Yes, it seems that an A Diminished chord fits right in, so you indeed could play an A Diminished. So, if A Minor works and A Diminished works, what about an A 4th? The notes are A-D-E, so it seems that it works too!

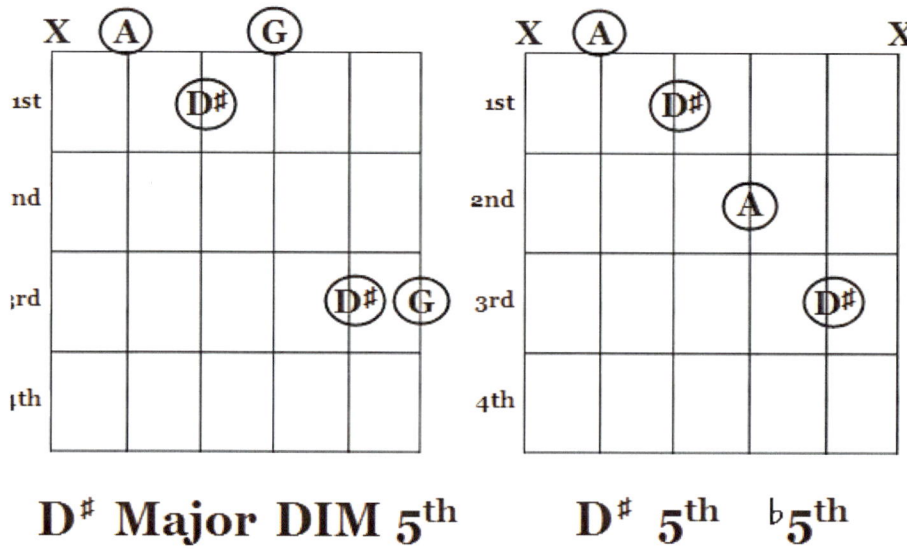

So, we have, A-C-E (A Minor), A-C-D♯ (A Diminished), and A-D-E (A Suspended 4th). And let's not forget the A 5th with the Suspended 3rd. All of these chords fit into the Blues scale, making an A Diminished 5th chord and an A 4th very nice flavoring to add into your blues progressions.

The C Major or C 5th chord is next in the progression. We can also add the C Suspended 2nd chord in for flavor. As well, the C Suspended 4th might add a nice tonal difference.

X = Mute to Deaden, or Try Not to Play

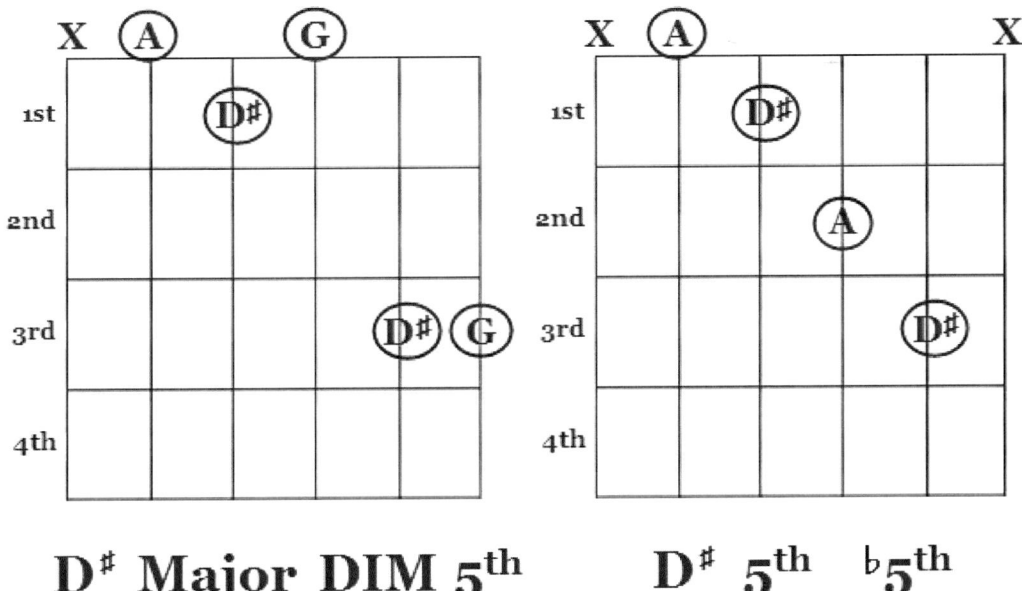

D♯ Major DIM 5th   **D♯ 5th ♭5th**

X = Mute to Deaden, or Try Not to Play

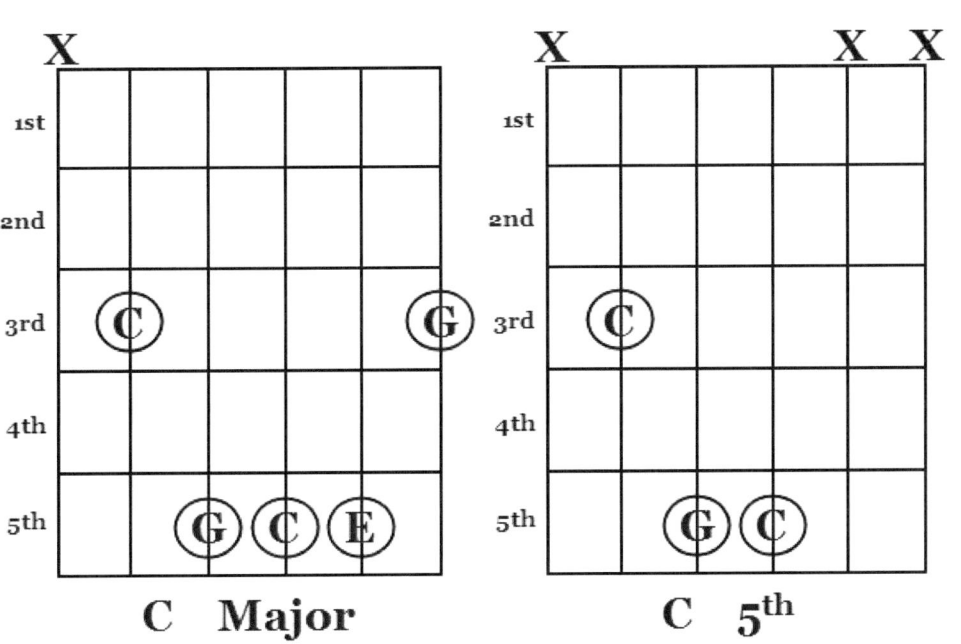

C Major   **C 5th**

78 | A LESSON A WEEK: *The Theory of Guitar Made Easy*

Here is where the Blues, as you are noticing, has a chance for much more flair than just a Pentatonic scale, and marks the true difference between a Les Paul versus a lot of pretenders to the throne.

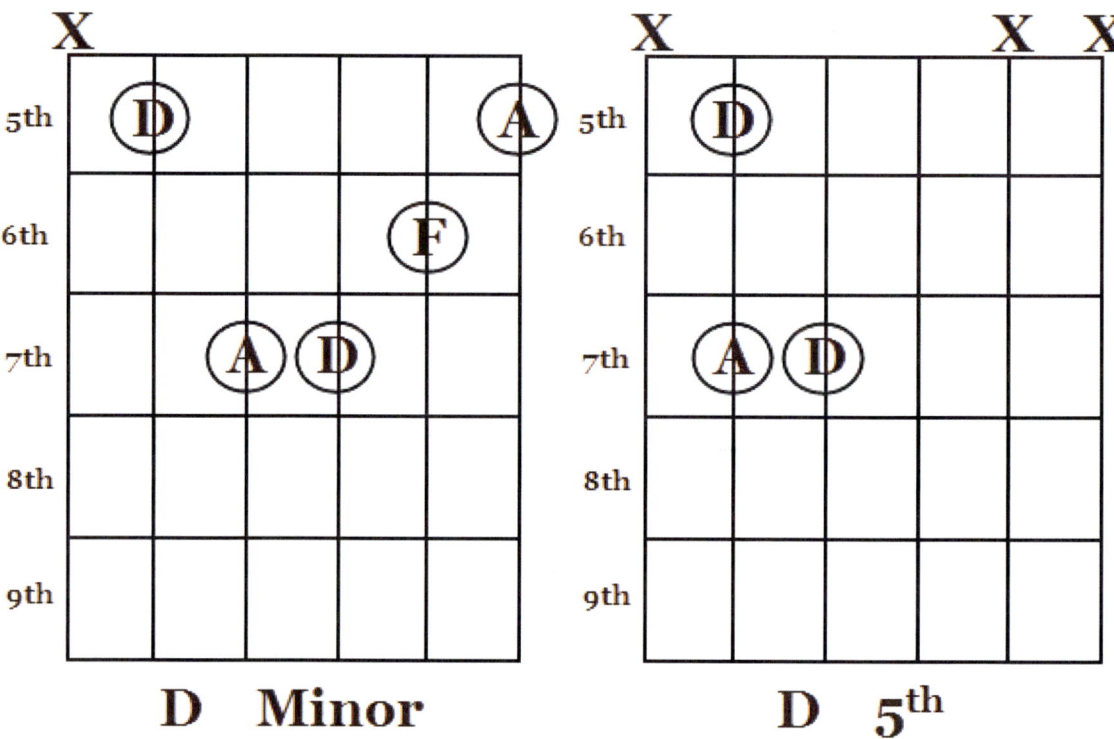

Now, let's look at the D and D♯ chord variations. This is where we will have maybe a little trouble understanding the chromatics to follow. First, we see that the D Minor would fit, as well as the D 5th, but if we are doing the D♯ chromatic in the chord pattern, we might want to be careful with the Suspended chords we use. However, if you apply what you've learned, you'll notice that the D Suspended 2nd chord is an excellent run to the D♯ ♭ 5th.

HUH? The D♯ ♭ 5th is the D♯-A-G notes, so you can see that the Blues can get into some funky chords and voicings. For example, you could just play a walk down between the D and the D♯ Roots from the D Minor chord, which walks down from the Roots or 5^{th}s to the 6th. This is very popular in some forms of the Blues. Mostly because of the use of the Root, 2nd, 3rd, 5th, and 6th of the Major C scale. (Root, ♭ 3rd, 4th, 5th, and ♭ 7th of the A Minor scale with the ♭ 5th added in for tonic flavor.)

I know, this is extremely confusing, and why I saved all of this for the last chapter of the book. Most believe the Blues and Pentatonics to be the basics and extremely easy to learn. If you take it as just Pentatonics and never learn the true theory behind it, sure, it is! But, if you study true theory behind Pentatonics and the Blues, you can see that it is the most complex of all playing. Yet, it is the most flavorful tones, and, like Jazz, can encompass so much more.

Now, let's look at the E Minor, or E 5th, and the G Major or G 5th. It suffices to stick to the Minor, the Major, and the 5th of each for these two chords.

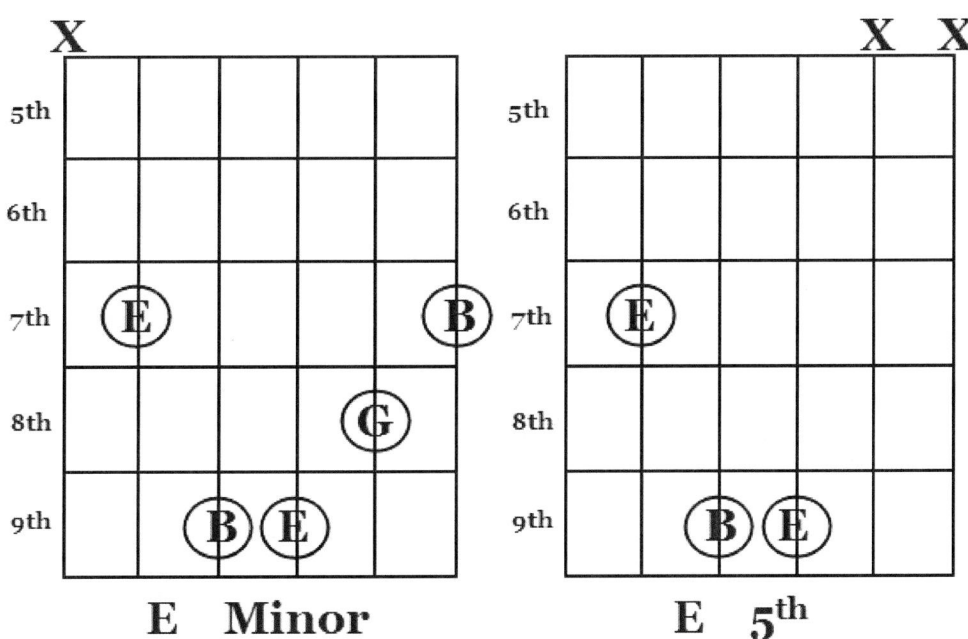

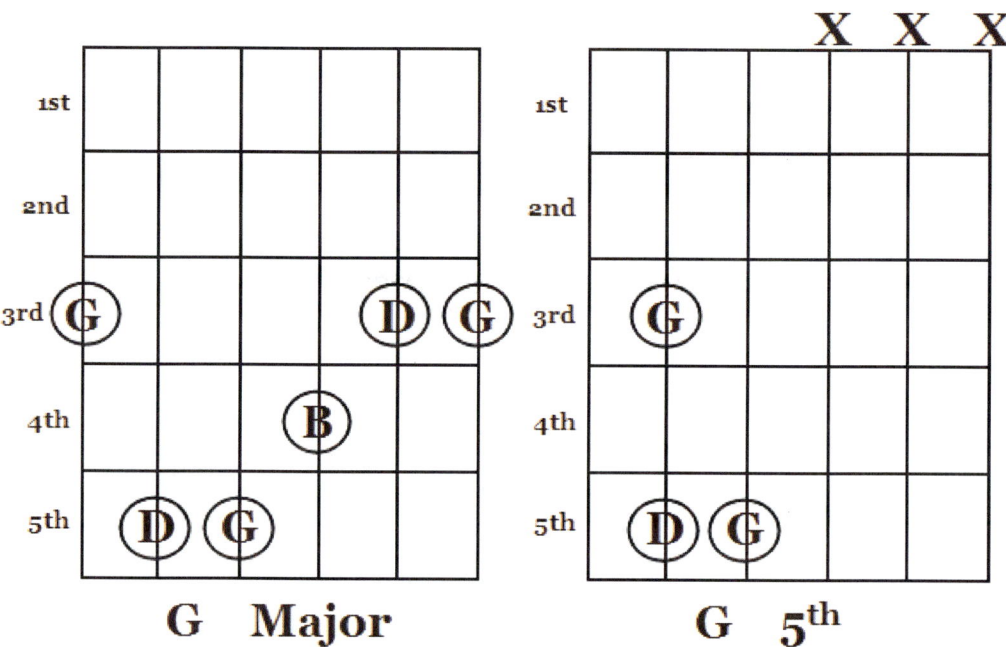

In ending, I like to say that I rounded off just a basic list of chords to use in Blues progressions, when in actuality, we could really write an entire book on just the Blues.

Study these unique patterns as applied to the Blues so that you can see the difference between the Blues and Pentatonics before moving onto the next week, where we'll dive deeper into Pentatonic scales.

WEEK FOURTEEN: BASIC PENTATONIC SCALE PATTERNS

This week, we'll cover some basic Pentatonic progressions with some basic Pentatonic scales to add to your repertoire. Remember before moving on that the Pentatonic scales come in two versions, the Pentatonic Major, with the Root, 2nd, 3rd, 5th and 6th and the Pentatonic Minor, with the Root, $\flat 3^{rd}$, 4th, 5th and $\flat 7^{th}$.

Basing the Pentatonic Major off of the C Major, we would have, C, D, E, G and A. Basing the Pentatonic Minor off of the A Major scale, we would have, A, C, D, E and the G, when we flatten the 3rd and the 7th. You should note that the only difference between the two scales are the starting point roots. If you're ready, let's dive into our work for this week.

First, let's look at a 1-4-5 Chord Progression, such as C, F and G, which contains all Majors or 5^{th}s. (A lot of Pentatonics are easier to start out with a 5th.) Playing the A in that progression would add a tonic Minor sound that might work at times, but would change the actual use of the Pentatonic. So, let's just try the basic scale, while chugging along with the chords.

Next, let's try a 1-2-5 Progression, such as C, D and G. Remembering the D chord is actually D Minor, where the other two are Major, which are the C and the G. Or, again, we could make it easy to just play the 5th chords instead...and in Pentatonics, we alway try to make it easy. Now, chug the chords along, playing the Major Pentatonic over it.

Note: Let's always remember to please transpose these scales and chords accordingly to what sounds good to us. Don't forget that we kept everything in this book based around the C Major scale and its derivatives to make learning guitar theory as simple as possible. Once you learn the math of theory, you can transpose the patterns and chords to ANY key! I personally always hated when a method book mixed up scales and modes and wanted you to do the work of knowing where and how it actually derived into the Major scales. Which is why I thought I would make it simple if I kept everything in one basic key, so we could see all the tonic differences, and we could then transpose to whatever scale we wished as we gained the knowledge of how they all were in reference to the Major scale we were transposing to from the key of C. Now, back to our studies...

With the Pentatonic Minor, we will use the same basic 1-4-5 and 1-2-5 patterns for our lesson. So, we have the A-D-E and A-B-E chord patterns, remembering that the A, D and E are all Minor chords and the B is the Diminished chord. Even if we play the 5th chords to make it easy, we still want to play the B Suspended flatted 5th (with no 3rd like all 5th chords). Just do the same playing the basic Pentatonic Minor scale over both for now to get use to its tonic flavor.

Now you will notice that IF we play the 1-4-5 in Pentatonic Major and the 1-4-5 in Pentatonic Minor, the progression in Pentatonic Major is all Major chords (the C, F and G) and all Minor chords in Pentatonic Minor (the A, D and E). The reason for this, was of course, to make the Pentatonic versions of the Blues as simple as possible. A vast cry from the actual Blues, which we will go into in next week's lesson.

For the rest of this week, play with these Pentatonic progressions, both Major and Minor, to commit each pattern to memory. If you are finding that your knowledge of theory has already vastly improved, feel free to experiment with transposing from the key of C Major to work with other Pentatonic patterns in other keys. Regardless, learn your Pentatonic scale patterns and I will see you in a week.

WEEK FIFTEEN: MIXING IT UP WITH BLUES SCALES

For most guitarists, mixing up the Blues (with Pentatonics) is a natural event. However, in this lesson, we are going to try to put a little theory behind it, to see what we would come up with for an innovative take on the Blues by mixing both the true Blues scales with the Pentatonics. First, let's look the three scales in the key of C Major, the Pentatonic Major, Pentatonic minor, and the Blues scale, in the diagram below:

Key of C Major	A		C		D	Eb	E			G
Pentatonic Major	6th		R		2nd		3rd			5th
Pentatonic Minor	R		b3rd		4th		5th			b7th
Blues	R		b3rd		4th	b5th	5th			b7th

As you can see, the Pentatonic Major is made up of the Root, 2nd, 3rd, 5th and the 6th. The Pentatonic Minor is made up of the Root, b3rd, 4th, 5th, and the b7th. The Blues is made up of the Root, b3rd, 4th, b5th, 5th, and the b7th.

By studying the variations between the three, you can see that the closest scales that seem related would be the Pentatonic Minor and Blues scale. But, let's look at the notes again for all three scales, in order.

First, we have the Pentatonic Major with C (Root), D, E, G, and A. Next, we have the Pentatonic Minor with A (Root), C, D, E, and G. I do hope you remember that both scales are actually using the same notes, only in a different mode.

Now let's stick with the Pentatonic Minor to keep the same Root as the Blues scale. With the Blues scale, we have, A (Root), C, D, D♯, E, and G. Wait, did you see it? There is NO difference between the three scales, except the chromatic run in the Blues scale by adding a b5th, to the scale.

So, why do most guitarists leave out the b5th? Because it is the actual chord progressions that are affected by adding the b5th and Diminished chords come into play. So, to understand how this can affect your playing, let's try the b5th in the Major Pentatonic scale, by adding a Blues Chromatic run: C, D, D♯, E, G, and A.

We now seem to have a problem of actually playing a b3rd in a Major run. It is a real problem, since when we play it, it adds a new flavor that sounds interesting and unique. The problem is audibly apparent by the chords we played the scale over, hence why the Diminished chord could come into play.

So, let us try adding the Diminished 5th in the 1-4-5 Minor progression. By adding in the Diminished 5th, we now have A Minor, D Minor, D♯ Diminished 5th, and E Minor chords, playing our Blues scale over it starting with a Root of A. Give it a try. I'll wait, ha-ha.

Now, we could just play the Pentatonic Minor, and yes it would work; but listen to the added flavor the actual Blues progression plays into it. Try this with other progressions, like the 1-4-5 of the Major progression, which gives us the C Major, F Major, and the G Major, adding again the D♯ Diminished 5th, and playing both the Root A Blues and Pentatonic over it. As you practice these various progressions between the three scales, you can see how you can create interesting flavors.

Spend this entire week working with the three scales and review the notes from this week before moving on to your final review. On this note, I will leave you now and hope that I have helped you to achieve a better look into more than just playing your guitar, but the actual theory behind your playing. Thank you ever so much for sticking it out and studying hard. Use this material to help you grow as a guitarist whether you're working on your own or studying with a teacher. I will see you in the next book.

WEEK SIXTEEN: REVIEW

Alas we've reached our last review. Answer the questions below. I HIGHLY suggest that once you've finished this review, you go back and revisit ALL the Review weeks in this book, which is why I've added a Final Book Review in the next section. Commit to memory what you've learned by experimenting on your guitar. Then, take what you've learned and apply it to your own playing to become a better player. Here are your final review questions:

- What is the difference between actual Blues and Pentatonic scales?
- Name the one note difference between the Pentatonic Minor and the Blues, which is a Minor Scale, when both are starting with the same root.
- Which scale out of the Blues and Pentatonics incorporates the Diminished chord as a useful voicing?
- What are some key chords to be used in the Pentatonic Scales for both Major and Minor?
- What are some key chords to be used in the Blues Scale? Which chord is Minor?
- What is the key difference between the Pentatonic Major and the Pentatonic Minor?

BOOK REVIEW

Alas, you've finished your 16-Week study course. I truly hope you enjoyed learning as much as I enjoyed teaching. Refer to this book often to maintain your basic guitar theory knowledge. But, the best way to retain this knowledge is through practical application by playing your guitar. Study this Book Review until you can answer every single question correctly:

CHAPTER ONE
- What are the open string notes on the neck of the guitar?
- What are the natural notes on the neck of the guitar?
- What is the difference between a whole-step and a half-step on the neck of the guitar?
- What is the difference between a whole-step and half-step in scale theory?
- What notes make up a chord?
- Where are the C Major scales and notes on the neck of the guitar?
- What note does each of the modes start with in the C Major scale?
- What positioning does each of the modes start with?
- What chords go with the C Major scale?
- What modes correspond with the C Major scale?
- What does the Do-Re-Mi pattern have to do with the Major scales?
- How do you transpose the C Major scale up an octave or two on the neck of the guitar?
- Which notes have Sharps and Flats, and which don't?
- Which sharps and flats are the exact same note?
- How do you play the different modes on the neck of the guitar?

CHAPTER TWO
- How do you suspend a chord?
- What is a power chord?
- What is the G power chord?
- What is an arpeggio?
- Which three notes make up the C Major arpeggio?
- What is the Circle of Fifths?
- How far away from a natural note is the sharp of that note?
- Which note would you add to make a C Suspended 2nd and which note would you remove?
- Name all the power chords in the C Major scale?
- Transpose the chords in the C Major scale to D Major.
- Name all the power chords in the F Major scale?
- Which three notes can be used to flavor any C Major progression when using the C and G Major scales, to segway into the change of scales?
- What makes up the D Minor arpeggio and note positions? (Ex: 1st, 2nd, 3rd, 4th, etc..)

- What is meant by a natural 5th?
- What other note is A♯ a substitute for?
- What natural note could E♯ be represented by?

CHAPTER THREE
- What note would you start with for the Dorian mode in the key of C?
- What is a C suspended chord, also known as a C 5th chord?
- What is the benefit of playing suspended chords?
- What is the difference between an A Aeolian and an A Harmonic Minor scale? What is the difference between the two scales?
  What is the one note that is changed in the C Major scale and all of its modes to make all of its scales and modes Harmonic Minor?
- Is there a difference in the Melodic Minor ascending and descending, and if so what is it?
- How many true Diminished scales are there that are not the same exact scale starting with a different root?
- What do you do to create a Chromatic scale?
- How many notes are in a true Chromatic scale?

CHAPTER FOUR
- What is the difference between actual Blues and Pentatonic scales?
- Name the one note difference between the Pentatonic Minor and the Blues, which is a Minor Scale, when both are starting with the same root.
- Which scale out of the Blues and Pentatonics incorporates the Diminished chord as a useful voicing?
- What are some key chords to be used in the Pentatonic Scales for both Major and Minor?
- What are some key chords to be used in the Blues Scale? Which chord is Minor?
- What is the key difference between the Pentatonic Major and the Pentatonic Minor?

ABOUT THE AUTHOR

Vince Inchierca (Ciampi) was born and raised in Revere MA, adopted by his maternal grandparents.

His interest in music started at the early age of four, with instruction in piano, trumpet, percussion, and music theory. By the age of twelve, he was a member of the Revere High School band, playing percussion, singing, and playing bass or keyboards in punk, rock and pop projects.

His music career as a guitarist began in 1987 with Hair Metal band *Blue Tiger*, who headlined almost every major club in New England from Boston to New York, Rhode Island, Connecticut, and more.

Having become disenchanted with the direction of music by the the early 90s, he went on to to study engineering, physics, computers, drama, and music. Fifteen years after Blue Tiger disbanded in early 1991, their Internet fan base created a MySpace account, which landed them a record deal with Retrospect Records, leading Blue Tiger to winning the 2007 AAM Glam Album of the Year award in Hollywood, California for their previously unreleased album, *Untamed Spirit*, which is still available on Retrospect Records in their top seller list.

By 2011, Vince embraced music again by reuniting *Blue Tiger* for a special performance at Rocklahoma 2011. After taking another year to work through what direction his music would take him, in 2012, while playing the Foxboro Event for the Narcissus Show (a benefit for Tom Brady's Charity), Vince realized a new vision and formed his new band, Shattered Nitemares.

His musical vision is now focused on writing and recording a new CD with Shattered Nitemares, while also teaching guitar, writing books, and performing. Vince is also a veteran who was also honorably discharged from the USMC.

www.ingramcontent.com/pod-product-compliance
Lightning Source LLC
Chambersburg PA
CBRC091505220426
43665CB00007B/82